This book is a must-read if...

❖ you want to take inspiration from philanthropist and community champion, Andrea Malam BEM;

❖ you want to explore the history of Anglo-Indians;

❖ you want to immerse yourself in what it means to be Anglo-Indian;

❖ you are interested in family history, memoirs and memory;

❖ you want to learn about the Anglo-Indian experience in different countries;

❖ you want to discover some famous faces that you had no idea were Anglo-Indian;

❖ you want to make a difference to your community and the world around you;

❖ you need positive thoughts about belief in yourself and your actions;

❖ you want to uncover the secrets of positive thinking, passion and determination.

What people are saying about Andrea...

"In a world where there are so many books being published every day, it is wonderful to find a book about Anglo-Indians across the globe. A community of individuals, who have learnt how to face challenges, learnt how to fit in but also learnt how to stand out from the crowd. Each chapter takes you on a journey with the highs and the lows. The chapters help you to understand what it is to be an Anglo-Indian as well as immerse you in their culture and history. A truly inspiring read."

Sonal Dave
Award-Winning Celebrant, Toastmaster,
Public Speaking Expert and Published Author

"Andrea and I met through a common contact in London and instantly clicked with our common beliefs and the zeal to help people. It was her dream to start a charity that serves children in need, and I latched on to it. I am now part of something she dreamed of and glad it happened this way.

All the very best for everything you have planned, Andrea, and keep giving it back to the society. We need more people like you!"

Conrad Vince
Trustee at Saving Dreams and financial services professional

This book is dedicated to all people
Anglo-Indian or of British Ancestry,
especially the Alexander family, the Raymer family,
and to all the contributors of this wonderful book.

Dreams Built on the Clash of Cultures

ANGLO-INDIANS ABROAD

Dear Vaishali

Best Wishes

Andrea

Changing Perceptions. Creating a New Heritage.

Andrea Malam BEM

First published in Great Britain in 2022
by Book Brilliance Publishing
265A Fir Tree Road, Epsom, Surrey, KT17 3LF
+44 (0)20 8641 5090
www.bookbrilliancepublishing.com
admin@bookbrilliancepublishing.com

A CIP catalogue record for this book is available
at the British Library.

ISBN 978-1-913770-48-8.

Typeset in Adobe Caslon Pro.
Printed by 4edge Ltd.

Contents

Foreword

The modern studies of the Anglo-Indian diaspora have focused on the experiences of Anglo-Indians in India before their immigration to the Commonwealth countries. In the history of modern post-colonial South Asia, the turning point for the Anglo-Indian minority was when India and Pakistan gained Independence and when policies of Commonwealth countries, such as Australia and New Zealand, allowed for the immigration of non-white inhabitants. Eventually, these events led to the large-scale migration of Anglo-Indians from South Asia to Commonwealth countries, spreading the diaspora throughout the world.

Anglo-Indians Abroad by Andrea Malam BEM investigates the post-colonial lives of the Anglo-Indians. They immigrated throughout history and narrate their stories of identity, migration, belonging and diaspora while touching the human elements of memory, food culture, and ambition.

The story of an Anglo-Indian woman's journey from Bombay to London and her journey to discover her ancestry and identity captures something in the zeitgeist. Andrea

Malam dives deeper into the history of her mixed-race ancestors, the Alexanders and the Raymers, right from the pre-colonial to the modern post-colonial times. She is documenting the journey from military service during the Anglo-Afghan Wars of the 1900s to leading the Royal Armed Force of Maharaja Sawai Madho Singh II of Jaipur State. Andrea extends her story to her relatives, documenting their journey in foreign lands which, in their way, are unique yet complex. These stories show how modern Anglo-Indian lives intersect with their identity.

The vivid description of Bombay through the 1970s and 1980s paints an image of a bygone era with that of a globalised image of Mumbai. While using the word Mumbai, the author has merely indicated a geographical location; however, while using the term Bombay, an emotion of home is radiated through the detailed description. While several stories describe the longing for home, they carried their home in their hearts and souls. Andrea Malam also highlights the professional history of Anglo-Indians, their presence in Civil Services, the nursing profession, and professional sportsmanship.

Joseph Oliver unfolds how White British people view the British who identify as Anglo-Indian; the critical question of race and its place in modern Britain. Oliver ultimately recounts how Anglo-Indians come to a consensus on their identity in modern times. Lyn Tyler views childhood memories of Anglo-Indian parents and lives in colonial Bombay through their narratives. The story of Keith and Philip Alexander and their journey from Mumbai to London through professional sports and balancing their new lives in the United Kingdom is a testament to the immigrant struggle.

The story of Lesley-Anne Raymer highlights the Canadian experience of Anglo-Indians, and her commitment to educating and creating a place for her identity in the Canadian lands shows the strong association of Anglo-Indian identity. The chronicles of Anglo-Indian engineer and professor Blair Williams in the United States is nothing less than a story of American dreams and a commitment to give back to the community in India through the 'Blair and Ellen Williams Education Trust'. The story of Blair Williams is one of the rare accounts of Anglo-Indians in the United States. Not only does Williams recount the story in America, but also compares it to his experiences in India and England.

Andrea Malam and her commitment to society and philanthropy are beyond commendable. Her service to diversity and inclusion in UK Law Enforcement, and her charity work at Saving Dreams, earned her several accolades, including the British Empire Medal by Her Majesty Queen Elizabeth II.

This work is well narrated and researched, using stories of Anglo-Indians from the United Kingdom, Canada and the United States of America and the stories of Anglo-Indians. They have relations with these Commonwealth countries. These stories are sensitive and evoke a sense of emotion toward the Anglo-Indian community residing outside. *Anglo-Indians Abroad* is a significant contribution to the range of diaspora stories – the vivid imagery of Mumbai when it was Bombay, the dilemmas and outcomes of Indian Independence, the nature of a hybrid identity, food culture, and at heart, a sense of home. References are made to the Europeanised lifestyle of Anglo-Indians in Mumbai and Jaipur.

Other critical aspects of Anglo-Indian identities, including Christianity, accent and language, are referenced in the wake of social bonds, ideological binding of the international community, and the professional lives encompassing the lives of younger Anglo-Indians. While the memories of the Anglo-Indians beyond the Indian shores fade, the need to preserve their stories is vital; the younger generation has to ask themselves who they are and where they belong in terms of their race and identity. *Anglo-Indians Abroad* is one such critical attempt to document this gap in stories.

Vishwajeet Deshmukh
Lawyer and Historian of South Asia
Mumbai, India
vishwajeetarnav@gmail.com
Twitter: @vishwajeetda
Instagram: @vishwajeetarnav

PART ONE

1.

Introduction

Where do I get my Inspiration from?

Do not go where the path may lead.
Go instead where there is no path and leave a trail.

*Mother Teres*a

Mother Teresa has always been an inspiration to me, because of her motivation to make a difference to the lives of others. She dedicated her life to helping those that were less fortunate. Mother Teresa was the Catholic nun who dedicated her life to caring for the destitute and dying in the slums of what was then called Calcutta – now known as Kolkata.

Her service to others continued after her death and people began invoking her intercession to assist them when they were ill. Mother Teresa's miraculous cures were investigated by the Roman Catholic church and in recognition of her first miracle, she was beatified in 2003. She was canonised on 4th September 2016, as Saint Teresa of Calcutta. This goes beyond leaving a legacy, and I'd like to achieve a similar story of making a difference in the lives of others when I look back on my life.

I believe sometimes the smallest of gestures make the biggest difference. It costs nothing to smile, yet this small act can have a big impact. This principle drives me to do whatever I can whenever I can for others because I want them to feel happy, appreciated, and loved.

There was a time in my life when I felt unhappy, unappreciated, and unloved. The greatest change occurred when I became a mother. It was no longer me who I had to focus on, but my children. Even though I loved them, like many women, I began to lose who 'Andrea' was and her dreams dissipated into the ether. This is the sacrifice many women make when they choose motherhood.

Without realising the personal exchange for the blessing of becoming a mother, for me and many women, the joy soon turns into a challenge. The fear of admitting that you may lose your identity, your sense of self and that perhaps motherhood is not everything women perceive it to be, floods mothers with guilt.

The mundane routine that being a parent brings can often leave you feeling underestimated, unloved, and taken for granted. Experiencing such pain is something I do not want others to feel if I can help it. Having been brought up in India, my lifestyle taught me to think of others as a member of a large family.

Someone once said to me,

"Andrea, grow your own way. Make your own path, have your own identity. Be You! Be Yourself! Be true to yourself! Believe in yourself!"

Here were the words being said to me that I would say to others. It hit me like a ton of bricks: I always put how others felt before my own feelings. What is the safety advice they say on airplanes? Put your own mask on first before helping others.

Never a truer word was spoken that struck to the core of my very being.

Despite being proud of all my achievements and all the acknowledgements I received, I always asked myself if these achievements defined me as a person.

Was I a change-maker?

Was I an achiever?

Was I confident?

Was I making any difference?

I was not sure, until the following experiences forced me to look at who I was becoming and who I was at that time in my life.

❖ In 2017, I received the Queen's Medal for Long Service and Good Conduct within Law Enforcement.

❖ In 2018 I was awarded the Diversity Role Model award in the National Crime Agency (NCA).

❖ In 2022, the Queen's New Year's Honours List mentioned my name. I was awarded a British Empire Medal (BEM) for services to Law Enforcement in Diversity and Inclusion.

It appeared that good fortune was raining down on me in recognition of the last three decades of my life.

If the aforementioned honours were not enough for one person, still crossing my path was the Honorary Doctorate I was awarded in Humanities for my part in community and charity work as the Trustee of Saving Dreams, my charity for underprivileged children.

These were tokens of true honour that I now had to recognise and believe that the work I was choosing to do was truly meaningful and making a significant difference in the lives of others. The realisation is quite astounding yet humbling.

My dream of making a difference for others around me was starting to become a reality. One small step can change the whole course of one's life. When you find a purpose and connect to who you are, then you begin to envision a better world and acknowledge your mission that drives you to get out of bed each day and follow your path. I can confidently say that I am building an empowering global community of courageous, diverse individuals, enabling them to feel connected, happy, and content.

It took me years to overcome the bias, bullying and gender gap in Inclusion, Diversity and Equality. Now I am a Leader! Leading with Empathy – Believing in myself and following my dreams!

I want my story to be the reason someone else feels they can have a dream, build on it, and then see it come true. I have awakened to this blessing, and I now value it as a remarkable gift.

It's never too late to chase your dreams; follow and achieve your dreams.

My Anglo-Indian heritage is one of the facets of my life that makes me feel most proud. It is such a humbling honour to represent the people, culture, and heritage of Great Britain and India wherever I go.

When I decided to write *Anglo-Indians Abroad*, I was thinking about the Anglo-Indian culture and how I could contribute to the perceptions and beliefs around it and its quality to the rest of the world.

The hierarchy of culture; the authentic food; the mixed wardrobes of Western and Indian clothes; the mix of languages; behaviours and values; and last but not the least, the beliefs.

What I want the readers to experience and imagine are the movies conjured up by the incredible stories within this book.

Be Inspired! Be Influenced!

2.

The Anglo-Indian Story: A Short History Lesson...

From around the 18th to the early 20th century, the term "Anglo-Indian" referred specifically to British people working in India. The term as we know it today first appeared in the 1911 census of India, identifying mixed-race citizens as a distinct group from both Indians and white British/Europeans.

The Indian Constitution recognises Anglo-Indians as citizens of mixed Indian and European descent, and they were listed as a minority in 1950.

The British Raj (known as Direct rule in India) was the rule of the British Crown on the Indian subcontinent from 1858–1947. In 1946–47, as independence grew closer, tensions turned into terrible violence between Muslims and Hindus. In 1947, the British withdrew from the area, and it was partitioned into two independent countries – India (mostly Hindu) and Pakistan (mostly Muslim).

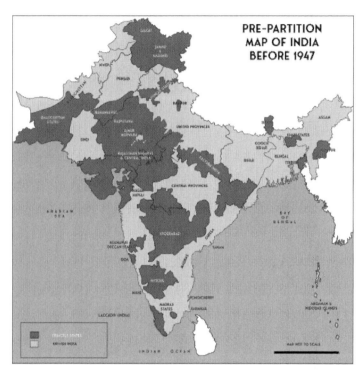

Old India (pre-1947)

New India (post-1947)

The Anglo-Indians were a mainly Christian community caught between two cultures. They spoke many languages, they adapted, and tried to get along with everyone, earning them the title of "fun-loving people" who enjoy life today no matter what tomorrow brings. They lived for the present day. Sometimes their fun-loving antics were misconstrued for being decadent; however, it did not mean they had no morals.

Throughout history and over a period of three hundred years, there were many Anglo-Indian Wars fought in the Indian subcontinent within the different states.

The first one of them was the Anglo-Mughal War, also known as Child's War. The others were Anglo-Mysore War, Anglo-Maratha War, Anglo-Burmese War, Anglo-Afghan War, Anglo-Sikh War, to name but a few. These wars led to the establishment of British colonial rule in India. Most of the key battles fought have proved to be very significant and impactful in the present-day culture of the Indian people. Their social status declined rapidly which resulted in many families leaving India.

Following Indian independence in 1947, Anglo-Indians seemed to suffer an early backlash and were looked upon as being different. At this stage, the Anglo-Indian population was about 300,000, but they started to disperse to other parts of the Commonwealth. As they were of Christian faith, it was an easy transition into a Western lifestyle. However, the most important factor was the fact that their mother tongue was English.

There was a time when the Anglo-Indian was considered as an opportunist and even a traitor to India. However, I believe that the Anglo-Indians were loyal to the British Raj before Indian independence and then later to the Indian Royal families too. Of course, like all communities, they have shortcomings and limitations. But Anglo-Indians were also a legal community, with qualities and responsibilities who were prepared to change and adapt to anyone and anything to better themselves. Evidence can be found in the vast amount of Anglo-Indians that have succeeded all over the world, including the United Kingdom, United States of America, Canada, Australia, and Ireland, to name a few. However, migrating to other parts of the world did not stop them from being interested in the life and family they left behind.

It's uncertain how many Anglo-Indians still remain in India. But current research says that the Anglo-Indian community is approximately 125,000 (https://www.britannica.com/topic/Anglo-Indian). Nevertheless, they are an important cultural group and bear a sizable chunk of Indian history.

The community that lives on in India continue to contribute to serve public services such as the railways, armed forces, law enforcement, hospitals, schools and even the local government. There have also been some great celebrities, sport stars and personalities too that you can read about later in Chapter 13.

An Explanation of the Caste System...

India and its caste system! The caste system classifies Indians into socio-economic groups, including upper- and lower-class common people. There are four broad categories: Brahmin, Kshatriya, Vaishya and Shudra.

3.

My Story: Going Back to My Roots

I was born in India, but the United Kingdom made me. Why do I say that?

In the late 1960s, a young, curious and fun-loving girl was born in the city of Bombay (now known as Mumbai), but years later moved to the United Kingdom.

As far as I remember, my father was in the Indian Civil Service and my mum had trained as an auxiliary nurse but was a housewife.

India is where I received the best start to convent-style school education which laid solid foundations for my later life.

England offered wonderful opportunities for my career choices building on my foundation and passion to make a difference. I believe I have the best of both worlds.

Just like my ancestors, and through many generations, working in the civil service was in my blood.

I have had a distinguished 25-year career in law enforcement working in several different roles, receiving Director General and Director Commendations for my work and commitment.

My role in the civil service was one of protecting the public, vulnerable children and women, and I have maintained those principles outside of the workplace after retiring in many charitable activities.

A few years ago, while being a chairperson of the Black and Minority Ethnic group at the workplace, I was fortunate enough to be invited to be a keynote speaker, where I spoke about my heritage and culture. I found this experience both nerve-wracking and exhilarating. It gave me a hunger to share my story more through speaking about it. Here I had opportunities to share my message and make a difference to those who heard it. Once you begin speaking, it appears that a domino effect takes place and more doors of opportunity open for you.

The theme was 'Culture and Heritage'. We were discussing heritage, and it soon became apparent that heritage can be confusing and unclear when you embrace more than one culture. It is still very vague, and people are still not sure about what being an Anglo-Indian means!

During the question and answer session, someone in the audience asked me a number of questions.

"Andrea, how would you summarise your heritage? What do you call yourself? What is an Anglo-Indian? Is it a race or is a culture?"

My response was easy.

"Being an Anglo-Indian is different. It's a community caught between two cultures and several languages, but somehow manages to accept and adapt by infusing the best of both worlds."

The little story that springs to mind, making me smile, is when my husband told his mother he had met this girl who was an Anglo-Indian. The response was to keep away from women like her! We had a reputation that was misconstrued. Her initial reaction reminds me of the phrase 'Don't judge a book by its cover'. Once she had met me and got to know me, her perception of me changed. My calm and accepting nature enabled me to look at such situations with a knowing smile.

It was winter 2021, just before Christmas and as the Covid-19 pandemic lockdowns were easing, I travelled to India. I usually make the trip every year. My sisters still live in India and I see them every year.

While in India, I had a thought. It was not uncommon for me to have lots of thoughts, but this one was different. My heart was thumping with excitement.

I had a compelling need to go down memory lane. It was like an itch. I needed to visit and familiarise myself with the place where I was born and baptised into Christianity.

"Let's go check out where we come from!" I blurted out to my three lovely sisters, Gillian, Donna and Janice (we were the Proud Alexanders!). "Let's go to the town and place where I was born and see if there are any Anglos still residing in the neighbouring areas."

Gillian was worried about it. She remarked, "Are you sure? It may be a bit emotional as it is not the same as when we were there."

Despite the concerns, our minds were made up.

Proud Alexanders was the name we gave ourselves every time we got together, especially with our cousin, Keith Alexander. I believe we adopted that frivolous yet strong title because we Alexanders were proud of our heritage and our culture.

So, the next day we made our way by Uber to the south of Bombay (now Mumbai). I am still getting used to calling it Mumbai, even though it has been changed for over 25 years.

Historically, the city changed its name from Bombay to Mumbai when regional political party Shiv Sena came into power in 1995. The Shiv Sena considered Bombay to be a legacy of British colonialism and preferred the city's name to reflect its Maratha heritage, hence renaming it to pay tribute to the goddess Mumbadevi. History also reveals that in the 16th century, the city was initially called Mumbai for the same reason.

Meanwhile, the Uber took us to the wrong side of the station, so we had to turn around, go over a bridge and back onto the right side. With the feeling of butterflies in my tummy, I shook at first trying to capture the visit on video, but was soon put at ease by my sister's smart idea.

Gillian, my elder sister of 16 years, made a running commentary as we reached Byculla, the area where I was born. She knew the area well enough as she was in her teens when we lived there.

Some of the discoveries we made included the Eugene Maternity Home where I was born, which has since closed. It's now used as a filming location for the famous Bollywood cinema. We managed to get permission from the watchman to go in and video the house. From a maternity home to a palatial home!

And how bemusing to find that the Khan Mansion, the house my siblings and I lived in, which has now become a government building. It was rather a strange feeling seeing it as an office and centre of government, no longer our home.

The only thing that still exists is the Gloria Church where I was baptised. I still remember the festivals that we attended in the church grounds during the 1970s. The pomp and glory in those days was exhilarating. The dancing and singing competitions brought many a smile to our faces. The competitions were mostly won by the Anglo-Indian families because they all knew how to do the dances: the jive, foxtrot and cha-cha-cha.

We finished the trip with a visit to the local Irani Cafe on the high street, for some delicious Irani chai and Maska Pau (a buttered bun). Despite it feeling a little strange for me, I am glad I did it because it rekindled happy memories and a warm feeling of nostalgia.

Encouraged and excited about my recent experience, I was keen to speak to some Anglo-Indians who still resided in India about how they felt still living there.

Some of the interesting replies were:

❖ "We are proud to say that we are Indians, and our constitution is the only one in the world that describes the Anglo-Indian as a minority."

❖ "We chose to remain in India because of our love for this country."

❖ "Anglos were trusted by the British to basically run the civil service in India. But unfortunately, the Anglo-Indians also believe that the British betrayed them and left them to the resentful Indians."

This perception may be the result of the British attitude towards the Anglo-Indian community or vice versa.

Anglo-Indians love to express themselves in music and dance. Singing was a real way of life for many. I still remember my dad playing the mouth organ; he was pretty good at it! Memories of my sisters singing at parties and cousins playing musical instruments, such as the guitar and drums, flood my mind. Some of these Anglo-Indians made a name for themselves in India while others travelled abroad to find their dream.

As mentioned, I was born in a small maternity home in Byculla in the south of Bombay, but my family moved around a few times. My siblings and myself went to different schools run by the Christian church at that time. My school only had about 40% children of Christian faith and the other 60% were made up of various faiths.

The caste system has created divides in my family. When my sisters decided to marry, my dad was very unhappy. In

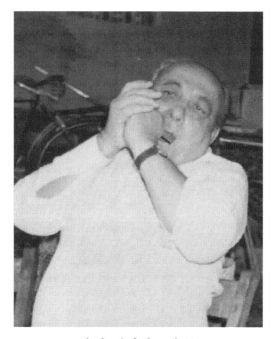

*Andrea's father playing
the mouth organ*

his view, their prospective husbands were of lower caste. This was one of the events that led to my departure from India, though there were many wounds that needed healing by that point.

We lived in neighbourhoods of shared traditions, making friends with all – Hindus, Muslims, Sikhs and Christians. There was no religion where sweets did not prevail. Our different cultural practices bought us together to be appreciated and enjoyed with each other. During their festivals like Holi, Diwali, and Eid, we would make sweets with them, and at Christmas time they would join us in learning Anglo-Indian recipes and vice versa.

Christmas Time in India

Mother: "Come on, my dears, it's December. It's the season of the Lord. The decorations need to go up and I need to start on the drinks and sweets!"

We knew then that it was December, and it was the Christmas month.

Christmas is universal and was always celebrated with past traditions, starting late November with the writing of Christmas cards for overseas and local addresses. The season was coming alive with the singing of Christmas carols, putting up lights and decorations in the local church and homes.

I also remember with great fondness the Christmas and New Year's dances that took place in the Christian Anglo-Indian community. These seemed to last the whole month of December and into the first week of January! As we didn't have much cooking equipment, we improvised, using our hands and cutlery found in the house. This was a time for sitting down and working out how to create things ourselves. We tried our hands at making doughnuts, Kulkuls (deep-fried pastry, shaped into curls), Christmas cake, Guava

Kulkuls

cheese, fudge, and homemade wine, all created with the traditional Christmas songs playing in the background.

The most interesting form of culture influx was around food with the Anglo-Indians having a distinctive taste in cooking cuisine. It was the amalgamation of European, British and Indian cuisines at their best. Various offspring of the British would adapt recipes as their preference of Indian food, by ensuring that not too hot spices were included in the dishes.

My favourite dish was called pepper water, a thin spicy soup made with onions and black pepper, and eaten with white or yellow boiled rice. Then there was the meatball curry, one of the mainstays, mulligatawny soup, trotters, and oxtail stew; not forgetting the famous traditional Christmas lunch! The roast meat, roasted potatoes, vegetables, the Christmas pudding – yes, we tried to have all the trimmings!

I do not make much Anglo-Indian food now but will make sure I have it when I go out to eat. Seeing an opportunity, one of my cousins has built a food business with his Anglo-Indian recipes.

Like most Anglo-Indian families, my family also have a long link and history with the civil service, railways, and uniform services. During World War II, Anglo-Indian women were the first to take up work in factories, offices and the nursing industry. This was not by choice, but because they had large families to support. This is what made them the backbone of the family and a pillar of strength and compassion.

We were raised in a developing country where opportunities to progress were scarce. There were chances for us to go abroad and to relocate but for various reasons, they were never taken. Most of our friends were clinging on to the English traditions but now it was becoming a diminishing culture.

After I finished my education, when I reached my early twenties, I decided I had to travel. I set off on the adventure and chance to get to know the rest of my family and make a difference to my life.

My association with the Anglo-Indian community faded when I moved to the UK and became involved in my married life and career. It's a sad situation back in India, as the remains of English legacy are diminishing and all I have left are the memories and black and white photos.

Our history is important. This was the reason I decided to visit my Anglo-Indian family and friends to get an idea as to why they left their roots and travelled abroad with the dreams and thoughts of a better life.

Dreaming of a better life is what brought me to the UK; I often wonder if it is the same for others...

Let's read their experiences and stories written in their words. Starting with my story, my experience, my legacy...

© Lyn Tyler 2021

PART TWO:
STORIES

4.

My Heritage by Andrea Malam BEM

"I've learned that people will forget what you said,
people will forget what you did,
but people will never forget how you made them feel."

Maya Angelou

The positive impact we make on the lives of others is so important to me. Inspiring others to follow their dreams, create a vision and take action to make it happen.

Nothing happens without a reason and this story is part of my life, my existence, my legacy! This is the story of both my paternal and maternal families.

The Alexander Family

There are no written records available as to when my British ancestors arrived in India, but it is believed it may be in the

1780s. Some were in the services of the well-known East India Company or were in the army of the ruling chiefs in the North and Central India.

My legacy started in 1919, right at the beginning and during the Third Afghan War, or the Third Anglo-Afghan War (6th May - 8th Aug 1919), when my great-grandfather Major James Alexander was one of those that led the Jaipur State Forces for the then Maharaja Sawai Madho Singh II (28th August 1862 - September 1922). The Maharaja was the adopted son of Ram Singh II, Raja of Jaipur.

It was said that Sawai Madho Singh II was presented a falcon by the Major, which he brought from Kabul after the 1919 war, following the assassination of Amir Habibullah, the Emir of Afghanistan. Why a falcon? I was curious so asked an uncle. He explained, "It was a status thing, Andrea," even in that era. The falcon represented freedom, victory, superiority and dominance. The Jaipur State Forces had just won a war for the Maharajas.

I was not surprised, as the status position still exists in many parts of the world. If you were a leader of the Royal Armed Force, I believe you were also practically considered a royal!

As my curiosity and intuition awakened me, I started doing my own research into the man who was my ancestor. I considered him an inspiration. But just who was my great-grandfather

I found out that Major James Alexander was of foreign origin. He was in fact a Scotsman but an Indian Rajput at heart. He came from a wealthy background and had achieved a fabulous military career.

The Alexander family in all its glory and splendours had

for generations served the Maharajas of Jaipur. Like me and the rest of my family, the Major spoke many languages, including English, Hindi, Urdu and Persian.

It is also said that the Major was held in high esteem and people would come from far and wide to listen to his stories and experiences. He was fondly called the "Storyteller of Ghat Gate" in Jaipur. Jaipur has many gates that are entrances to the city. One such gate was Ghat Gate, just near the Alexander residences. He would be surrounded by many people listening to his tales and experiences, laughing at his jokes and weeping at his tear-jerking historical stories.

The Major, like all other Anglo-Indians, was also a regular visitor to Halingar Hall in its heyday. Halingar Hall was the home of the Martin family until it was taken over for government use as part of the civil courts. There were elegant dances and exciting tombolas that preceded the grand dinners at the Hall, especially after his return from the Afghan War. Just picture the scene… the grandeur of the event, with huge rooms, high ceilings, and impressive chandeliers and candle lights.

Jaipur City in Rajasthan is known as the Pink City of India to many because of its pink walls and building structures. Sadly, I think it has now lost most of its glamour and history with the changes brought about by time. Most of the palaces have become five-star hotels. However, this city served as the capital of Jaipur state during the British Raj. The Alexanders' Jaipur residence on Agra Road was a flat-roofed bungalow (Bangla in Hindi) and outhouses on the land (Jagir). These originally belonged to the Jaipur Raj and were gifted to Major James Alexander one Christmas after his heroic role in the Afghan war.

The outhouses in the vast land were leased to other families and local businesses in the area. The Alexanders were the landlords (Zamindars in Hindi). This land was opposite the Central Jail constructed in around 1924. I can still picture myself looking at the Central Jail with its spectacular architecture just near Ghat Gate in Jaipur. We could see the massive walls surrounding the jail from the courtyard of our bungalow.

Sometimes memories allow us to relish in the past and revisit it as if it was yesterday. I was very fortunate to go and visit the house in my late teens. We travelled by train from Bombay Central to Jaipur Junction. I still remember sleeping on the veranda outside the bungalow on the charpoys (rope-thatched beds) under the stars in the scorching heat of over 40 degrees and seeing these odd containers inside the house.

"What are they?" I asked my uncle Harvey.

"Water coolers," he replied.

I had never seen water coolers before that trip. They were a type of cooling system that blew out cool air. I thought they looked strange but believe me, they did the job!

Sadly, the old structure of the house, a landmark of the olden days and outhouses, no longer exists. It has been replaced with new construction on the surrounding land. The house and area around it were sold to a transport and warehouse company a quarter of a century ago. It is now a fond memory to us.

Major James Alexander died in 1948 leaving behind a son, Thomas Henry Alexander, my grandad, who also served in the Royal Forces, and grandchildren, two of whom lived in the bungalow until their deaths while the rest migrated to other parts of the world. These included my great-aunt Marie Peyton (née Alexander) who lived to be over 100 years old, and aunt Sheila Bince (née Alexander, my father's sister), both in the UK. Then there was Colonel Ronnie Alexander of World War II fame in Australia and Vernon Alexander of sporting fame in India and then the UK. Both were my father's brothers.

My father, Wallace Alexander, and his brothers were well-educated and masters in their fields. Not forgetting my uncles, Harvey Alexander and Nobert Alexander, who lived in the Jaipur house until their deaths.

Major James Alexander –
my great-grandad

Enough said about my dad's side of family; now onto my mum's side:

The Raymer family

My mother was Phyllis Raymer. I did not know much about my mother's family as she had spent most of her school days and holidays in a boarding school in India, like most Anglos-Indians of that generation. It was the 'done' thing in those days for all children to be sent to a boarding school. Maybe it was the family tradition. "Not forgetting the discipline, think about the education that children get at boarding school," my mother said.

She had lost her mother (my grandmother) at a very early age and her siblings were much older. Her father, my grandad, was in the Indian Railways, so they had to move a lot with different transfers and postings. The only other relative I knew of when I was a child was her brother, Uncle Derrick as we knew him, and his family, who later migrated to Canada.

Post-Indian independence, every Anglo-Indian family had members heading off abroad, but not my father and mother, oh no. They were not interested in migrating. They stayed behind and got married! They had six children of which I was the last.

I had family on both sides settled around the world, some of whom I had no idea existed until recently.

Fast forward to…

20th July 2019, the day that changed my life.

It was a bright and sunny afternoon in the village of Bicester, in Oxfordshire. We were having drinks and some lunch.

"I have something for you," said a lady sitting across from me in the restaurant. In fact, there were three ladies in front of me that day. This lady was my cousin that I had never heard of until then. She handed me an envelope. Not sure what it contained, my hands trembled as I took it from her. It was like a scene from an old emotional family drama. The shock and surprise showed on my face when I opened it and saw my mother's handwritten Christmas and New Year greeting to her sister.

It said, "Dear Nesta, With our love & best wishes Phyllis, Wallace & fly."

There was a photograph of me at about two or three years old in my mother's arms, surrounded by my siblings. Tears rolled down my face. I was crying.

I had cousins. Not one, but five cousins! Ede, Lorna, Phyllis, Barbara and Gwen. My aunt named one of her daughters Phyllis after my mum! The afternoon was spent revisiting and reviving memories. This was just the beginning of my journey to find more about my maternal family and the long-lost cousins that I had not been aware of until that day.

This meeting of long-lost relatives reignited a spark of curiosity and the ensuing discovery once I did my DNA test and uncovered amazing connections through Ancestry.com. Each discovery brought me closer to my wider ancestry. I was a mixture of accent and cultures. I was Scottish. I was Irish. I was Welsh. My accent was, or still is, I believe, somewhat like a Welsh person born in India! In fact, I remember not too long ago, I was left a message to call a Welsh client who said to my colleague. "Please ask the Welsh lady to get back to me." This comment struck a chord with me.

When I first came to the UK in 1990, I did not know I had any relatives from my mother's side. To find out I had five cousins who were daughters of my aunt Nesta (my mother's sister) made me elated!

For a long time, I always felt unsettled about my identity. I am often made to feel different about who I am, my culture and my heritage. I felt I was never going to fully understand where I came from. It was only when I received the message from my cousin that the mystery started to unfold. I had maternal family I did not know existed not far from where I was in London.

Soon after that revelation, I found out that my mother had another brother called Hector who was in the army and fought in World War II. He was taken prisoner by the

Japanese. He never really recovered from being tortured and suffered from PTSD. He later came to the UK but never married and I believe passed away in 1974.

My dream of coming to the United Kingdom gave me other opportunities to meet members I did not know before from both sides of my family, such as my great aunt, uncles, and first and second cousins. You may think you know your family but when you start to ask questions and seek the answers, you discover new members of your family that you are excited to meet. During these meetings, you realise the depth and breadth of your family roots and the real heritage to which you belong.

My grandmother on the
Raymer side of the family

*My parents, Wallace and Phyllis Alexander,
with all of us children*

5.

Where are you from? by Joseph Oliver

"So, like, where are you from?"

She gazed at me interestedly, eyes glittering with sincere enthusiasm. Just a question, an innocent question. A question she had no doubt longed to ask from the moment she had first laid eyes on me. On my brown face, my dark – almost black – hair, my dark brown eyes, that to her mind clashed so discordantly with my English accent and name, which I had given her upon our first meeting, our first exchange of messages, all those months ago when we had both swiped right on each other's profiles and started talking.

She was a Literature grad, she liked knitted jumpers, she loved to go to theatre, and had been travelling around Europe and southeast Asia. She had two dogs and a whole cage (practically an aviary) of budgies, parakeets and parrots. She ticked so many boxes, I wondered if she was for real. She read the same books and the same newspapers – we'd

Joseph Oliver

even spent a whole late night talking about politics, which contrary to perceived wisdom, had ruined everything and we had found out that we seemed to be practically perfectly aligned on all key points of contention, even down to hypothetical candidates for the next general election. She was a real-life Mary Poppins – practically perfect in every way. But it had obviously been too much to hope for.

I mustered a smile and stared weakly back, trying to hide my dismay. Not that I was shocked by the question, or hadn't been half expecting it, but at the same time hoping that it wouldn't come up, because I wasn't. It was always going to come up. It was bound to come up. It always did with English people, with white people.

Despite conquering pretty much the entire known world (I think I'd read the startling, sobering fact that out of 300 or so countries that exist in the world today, only something like 22 had never been invaded by the British), they managed to get the paws of their grubby little Empire into every region in the world, so much so that the sun had never set on it. I found it both puzzling, tedious and downright cheeky that there was not only so little taught about the history of the British Empire and all the different peoples, citizens and subcultures that had been created as part of it and because of it, but that British people themselves were so utterly clueless about it. About anything and everything that wasn't two inches in front of their nose.

Not that I was against British people; I mean, I am British, aren't I? I mean, not only had I been born, grew up and lived here all my life, but Anglo-Indians were as British as you could get. I was perceived as proudly and staunchly British or Anglo-Indian; never Indian. I mean, I'd even imbibed a little bit of that myself, thinking of India as familiarly and as proudly as a fond extension of my family. A place to which we belonged, had come from, and had roots in, despite having never been there. Having roots in a community and knowing that there were others like you, despite that the place was more commonly associated with Sikhs, Hindus, Muslims and a variety of other faiths, peoples, regions, and demographics.

That was just the thing too – to my mind, and to pretty much all Anglo-Indians, the disconnect between being an Anglo-Indian and being an Indian was huge. It was vast, an enormous gulf, a gaping chasm. There was the world of difference. I would no more be able to associate myself with being Indian than I would with being from Belarus or China or Botswana. It was just totally alien to me. But I couldn't explain that to her; it would just never come across. This was just another of those times that I was fed up with it, of repeating myself yet again. The dreaded, inevitable question had reared its ugly head again.

It was a standard question that White British people probably asked everyone that didn't quite fit their preconceived notions of what people should look like.

My mind scrolled through the well-used and well-rehearsed answers that had come to form my standard, stock replies to this question, and I had developed a variety of answers that rolled off the tongue like melted butter off a slice of freshly toasted bread.

I could give her my hometown, where I had been born and lived my entire life, but that wasn't what she was after. I could say London, having spent the entirety of the weekends and school holidays of my childhood and teenage years visiting grandparents, aunties and uncles and cousins, and where I had recently moved to after graduating university and getting my first, desperately sought after, proper job, but that wouldn't satisfy her either.

I could refer to the Portuguese surname that had been my mother's maiden name before she married my dad and became a Reynolds. I could have referred to my dad himself and how he had started his life in Ireland before coming to university in England and meeting my mum on their first day in student halls; they had been inseparable ever since, settling down and having me, my brother, and my sister. Now that would really confuse her; I'd said it a couple of times before to a couple of well-meaning, but ultimately too pushy for my liking, colleagues at a previous job and it had worked a treat. I'd finished it off with a big smile and a look of feigned innocence and had to bite my tongue to stop from laughing at their faltered expressions as their expectations weren't met, which turned to confusion, and then turned to considering asking a follow-up question.

I quickly decided against it and ultimately giving up and rounding off with a tentative "... Oh... right.... That's... cool."

I could even refer to the Dutch, French and staggeringly even Jewish ancestry, of whose threads weaved and patterned their way into the dizzying, spiralling, rich and totally unique tapestry of the heritage on my mum's side of the family. But her question would still remain and she would still press on, undaunted, until she heard the answer that she wanted to hear.

She ploughed on relentlessly on what for her was a fresh, virgin path, having presumably never met anyone quite like me. She was from, and we were in, an overwhelmingly white part of the Home Counties, which at the last census had revealed itself to being demographically 97.8% White British, but for me it was well-worn, well-trudged, often visited territory. The questions, which were translated in a variety of ways, but that always emerged and manifested itself as, "You seem so English. Why are you brown?"

Plus, I didn't want to do any of those things; I liked this girl. I wanted her to get to know me and wanted to get to know her. Also, was it just me or did this happen to everybody? Was I being too over-sensitive, a bit of a snowflake?

When I reflected on it, all my cousins and even some of my uncles and aunties had married English people and it didn't seem that they had any sort of issue or found hiccups along the way. Not that I'd grilled them extensively on the nitty-gritty details of their courting and dating lives, but it just didn't seem to be something that I had ever heard of in any reporting back with frustration or having cropped up as a regular occurrence.

For goodness' sake, even my dad was white, and it never seemed to be an issue between him and my mum. And they'd met back in the sixties and seventies, when people used to be able to get away with spouting any old rubbish that they fancied and were much less sensitive about coming across as rude or prejudiced.

I decided that I would take one of the options that I hadn't taken with someone in a very long time. I wasn't going to deflect or dismiss or brush over the question. I was going to be open and go into detail, as much detail as I knew, as much as I could, and be completely and utterly honest about who I was, who I thought I was and who I had been led to believe I was. I would take on the inevitable follow-up questions, the blank looks, the gaps in the knowledge, and explain as faithfully and as intricately as I could about who I was; an Anglo-Indian.

I steeled myself and tentatively, delicately, poked my toe into the water.

"Do you know what an Anglo-Indian is?"

Cue the blank look, the look of confusion, the words erupting from my lips and landing with a crash on her ears, roaring and tumbling down her ear canals and clattering around inside her head as she pedantically, ploddingly rummaged around inside her brain for a frame of reference, a previous bit of knowledge, a clue, anything. She was having no luck. Her eyes, skimming and darting in that momentary fit of concentration, flicked back to meet mine.

"No…"

I take a deep breath and prepare myself for the next step. I put the rest of the foot into the icy, shockingly cold water. This isn't one you can just splash into and hope for the best. It requires delicacy. Tact. Finesse.

"Well, you see, it's like…"

Her eyes light up as she strikes upon something in her head. A light bulb has gone off. She thinks she's found what she's looking for. It seemed to be a perching moment, a burst of clarity. All she's waiting for is for me to confirm it for her.

"So, like you're Indian, but you grew up in England?"

She beams with pride as if she's suddenly understood, and we are on the same plain of comprehension. As if we are two safe breakers who have finally cracked the code of some illustrious bank and are now mutual elites, comrades in arms. Like she has become privy to and invited into an exclusive arena, unknown to all but a select, worthy few.

My expression remains the same – I do not betray anything as to how I am feeling. OK, it's not the strongest start and not in an ideal world how I would have wanted it to go, but I am sure it's nothing that can't be easily explained away.

I arrange my face in what I hope is an expression of warm invite, the kind a teacher might give to a pupil who they are especially trying to encourage to participate more in class and don't want to shatter their confidence in putting their hand up and answering class questions.

"Ah, not quite…" I hear myself say. However, the cogs in her head have been set in motion and there is no stopping them – she is now firing on all cylinders, determined to get to the bottom of the mystery.

"Angola… Angola-Indian? That's in Africa, right? So, is that like half-African, half-Indian? And like you're Indian, but…"

I can see that this is going wildly off course, like a novice skier who has managed to leave the relative safety of the slope and has now found themselves slaloming erratically off-piste, narrowly avoiding hostile branches and roots and rocks except for a well-timed lift of the ski or a tuck in of flailing arms. Looking to steady the ship, I scrabble frantically for a short, sharp, resolute pop culture frame of reference that will calm the storm, something that will permeate the maelstrom that has been churned up inside her head and will hopefully both reset and bring it to a close.

"Do you know the singer Cliff Richard?" I cry out desperately.

She stops, mouth open and poised to speak. I look at her eyes. The name does the obligatory circuit around her synapses. Neurons fire and crackle. Somewhere, she has found a match. She recognises the name.

"Have you heard of a singer called Cliff Richard?" I press on, seeming to have a foothold now. A calm but firm steer in the right direction.

"Yes, I have!" she replies.

OK, finally a step in the right direction. I nod my head and smile.

"Ah, cool. Yeah, well he's an Anglo-Indian."

"Really?" She looks surprised. "I just thought he was English?"

I remind myself that Rome wasn't built in a day, that mighty oaks from tiny acorns grow and push on, undaunted.

"Did you have fun?" my mum asked, pushing a glass of water and a plate of dinner towards me. Mince curry, with lentils, rice and kale – my favourite.

To be honest, any meal that was anything other than curry and rice was met with slight disappointment. I'm not knocking other cuisines, but there is nothing that beats curry, especially not the way my mum and aunties and uncles make it. My nana's jungli pilau is hands down the best food I ever have or ever will taste. I had seen English people or guests come round for dinner and pick themselves a knife and fork as their cutlery to eat with, and it never failed to leave me aghast. It was barbaric, practically primitive. The correct way is, as every Anglo-Indian knows, with a spoon and fork pairing. I tucked in, hungrily.

"She kept asking me where I was from."

My mum laughed and looked at me with a smile. I always filled her in about the most important aspects of my life and had regaled her with stories that ranged from the absurd to the downright dumb. "Same as always, eh?"

"Well, it would just be nice to find an Anglo-Indian girl that I don't have to go through this whole rigmarole every time," I splutter thickly through a mouthful of kale, dhaal and rice. "I wouldn't have to say anything. Not a word." I swallow fully and carry on eating, piling up a mouthful onto my spoon. "How come you ended up with Dad? I'm guessing he never asked you 'So why are you brown?' on a date."

"She didn't ask you that either, to be fair to her."

"Yeah, but that's what she meant. Hold on," I suddenly think, brandishing my fork accusingly aloft as it made its way to my mouth loaded with food, "how come you've never had any Anglo-Indian friends?"

"We didn't know any. Nana and Grandad kept themselves to themselves."

"So, Nana and Grandad packed up their lives and moved themselves and all their kids to a new country and didn't think to stay in touch with anyone or be around people who would be like them? They didn't want to stay with any Anglo-Indians?"

"Grandad bought the house and we all lived there."

"But that's what I'm saying. From what I've researched, Anglo-Indians are found a lot in Croydon, South London. And you guys just pitched up in the middle of Camden, North London."

"There's Anglo-Indians everywhere."

"How come I've never met any?"

"All I know is as much as I have told you."

"But that's practically nothing, Mum. You were three when you left India and you've never been back since." I throw my spoon down with frustration. "I want to be with other Anglo-Indians, I want to know other people. All I've got is some far-off stories about how things used to be, and our family. I've got no sense of community, no sense of a group or a network or of belonging to anything. All I've got to say when someone asks me why I look like I do is 'Oh, ah, ummm, yeah I'm not Indian, but I am, but it's complicated, say have you heard of Cliff Richard?'!"

I look at my mum.

"I want to be able to walk in somewhere and everybody just knows, you know? There's no explaining, there's no questions, we are just all on the same page. I mean, we don't even know anything. Nana and Grandad never told us all anything and it doesn't seem that anyone else is really that interested. But I am!" I cry, "I want to know! I want to belong somewhere, instead of always feeling like the odd one out, like no one gets it."

I sigh and pick up my cutlery again. "I just want to be with other people, who are the same as me, Mum. I just want to be more in touch with who I am. Find out more stuff. Meet people. I just want to know."

I begin eating again resignedly, dejectedly, sadly. Mum comes over and gives me a hug, draping her arm over my shoulder. Normally I have to bend down to hug my mum, which invariably leaves her shoulder digging into my larynx, which isn't the most comfortable thing in the world, but sitting down we are more or less at an even height.

"Love you," she says.

"Love you too," I mumble back.

6.

An Anglo-Indian's Life in Mumbai by Richard Lloyd Raymer

I was born on 7ᵗʰ July 1960 to Anglo-Indian parents, Derrick and Marie Raymer, in what was then known as Bombay. My father left school at the age of 18 and went straight into the army along with some of his siblings, as part of the British Army in World War II. The end of the war and Indian Independence in 1947 saw most of Derrick's siblings leave India. However, Derrick decided to stay and transferred to the Indian Railways. Soon after, he joined a private mechanical company working on large industrial machines. My mother was a housewife who looked after the family and was very proud of all their achievements. Her hobby was cooking and feeding everyone that came to the house. She loved entertaining.

My three sisters migrated to Canada and my father joined them soon after my mother died about 15 years ago. Derrick

*Phyllis (Raymer) Alexander and her brother
Derrick Raymer in 1948, I believe, after the
Indian Independence.*

died in Canada in 2018. I decided to stay in Mumbai and make my life here.

I studied at St Peter's High School in Mazagaon, Mumbai, which was, and still is, a school that caters for the Anglo-Indian community. I have friendships that have lasted over 40 years, many of whom have ancestral homes in Goa and Mangalore.

At the age of 21, I travelled to London with my mother and sister to visit our extended Anglo-Indian family. This visit left me very upset. I found that all my mother's Anglo-Indian family lived in fear of a section of British youth known as skinheads, who were racist thugs. They called us 'bloody Indians' and terrible racists names that I cannot even mention. I was very frightened and traumatised by this as I had never experienced it before.

Back in Mumbai, working and partying gave me back my sense of identity and community. I learnt some Indian languages and loved Indian foods, especially the delicious street food on every corner! This gave me a true sense of belonging. Although I was not a financial big-wig, I became a travel agent and travelled all over the globe. The job allowed me to see a lot of India that I didn't know well, as well as many other parts of the world.

India is a beautiful place! When I travelled to countries such as Turkey, the Balkan States, Finland and Norway, and people realised that I was Anglo-Indian, it attracted a lot of interest and curiosity. I was often considered being from an 'exotic' country, but it is my country and I liked that.

In Mumbai, and in fact most of India, looking the way I do – my dress, speech and basic mannerisms – are all based on my Anglo-Indian upbringing. To this day, I am respectfully called 'Saab' or 'Saiba', and in most government offices and official channels I am called 'Sir' and saluted by the doormen at banks, hotels and the like. I like that as it makes me feel like a first-class citizen. Although I miss my siblings in Canada, life is not too bad here in Mumbai; in fact, with a substantial bank balance, it is pretty good!

I was once told by a great promoter of East Indian culture and foods, who also happened to be the editor of a local newspaper in Mumbai, that Anglo-Indians have lost their significance in this city. This got me thinking and sparked my passion for cooking my mother's great Anglo-Indian

Richard Lloyd Raymer, a few years ago

specialities which had never been shared with anyone. Many people had very little idea of what true Anglo-Indian cuisine was like; the tastes, smells and textures.

This prompted me to start the company, 'Rich Foods – Rich in Taste, Rich in Style' – authentic Anglo-Indian specialities, which included all mother's recipes, as well as some tips on these dishes from my sisters. We supply great roast dinners of beef and pork, tender and succulent, cooked in a delicious spice mix, accompanied by roast potatoes, root vegetables and gravy, as well as other dishes.

One year later, the name of my delicious different tasting Anglo-Indian style food has spread by word of mouth all over this city and beyond! Besides getting to know some older Anglo-Indians who know and love this true taste of Anglo-Indian food, and who order from my menu, my biggest patrons are people who love Goan or East Indian style food they usually have at home.

Living in Mumbai, I can proudly say I have done more for the recognition of our community by highlighting and talking about our unique food style. And in an ironic twist, my biggest promoter and fan is the very editor of the local newspaper who said Anglos had lost their significance!

I am proud to be an Anglo-Indian while calling myself an Indian-Anglo!

7.

A Child's Eye View by Lyn Tyler

My beautiful, glamorous, somewhat formidable aunty raged through the house like a tornado. I heard her call my name and felt the seismic shift as her anger rolled up the stairs. My crime? It was an innocuous piece of prose in my very best nine-year-old script with lovely little drawings adorning its border. Unfortunately for me, this was displayed on the wall of my classroom for Parents' Evening. According to my enraged aunty, informing the 'entire world' that my favourite food was her chicken curry, yellow rice, pepper water and chapatis was a secret never to have been broadcast. It was 1969 and this marked my rude awakening on how my family attempted to keep 'home' real whilst attempting to blend with their surroundings.

Home was India; more specifically, Bombay. Our surroundings were the industrial heartland of the UK's West Midlands. Travelling on the last voyage the P&O S.S. *Ranchi* made before going to the scuppers yard, my family arrived in 1951. I was born eight years later.

The irony, lost on my lovely aunty, was that while she was ensuring I understood never to talk outside the house about 'our food', her gold bangles jingled, and she looked fabulous in the 1960s minidress made from beaded fabric she had brought with her from 'home'.

I began taking more notice, beginning with our food. Kitchen windows were always firmly closed when she cooked and as soon as I could reach the kitchen counter, I had to help with the chapatis – not a single other child in my school knew what a chapati was, let alone how to make them. At 'AI' (Anglo-Indian) get-togethers or English parties with trusted friends, biscuit tins full of freshly made curry puffs would be consumed alongside the limp, dry-edged sandwiches.

Food was central to creating 'home'. Before Asian food stores began opening 20 miles away in Birmingham, my family booked a day trip to London at least three times a year to buy our spices, our sweets and, when in season, Alphonso mangoes. Creating a culinary home from home took some effort. My aunty wrapped each spice delight in copious amounts of newspaper to insulate the aromas, not wishing to assail the nostrils of our fellow coach passengers. I knew not to request school friends come to play, or 'come for tea', as they would smell our cooking. I thought this was such a shame – they were missing out big time on the delights of curry on toast and homemade spiced cutlets.

At around the same time, I began taking more notice of the difference in the homes of my school friends and of mine. Like many of them, we too had ornate Wedgwood dishes, cut-glass bowls and Royal Worcester porcelain ladies, but ours were sitting on intricately carved nests of tables next to highly decorated brass vases. These vases and tables, along with Indian fabrics, linens and homewares, had all been brought over in a large metal trunk that now served as my toy box. Our 'best' crockery had also been carefully transported from 'home', and leaning against our dining room wall was the tournament-sized Carom board that had been shipped over from India. Carom was a board game that everyone used to play in India. Above this hung a framed picture of the Gateway of India monument.

I knew the Gateway was a special place. My family had grown up on Apollo Bunder, also known as Wellington Pier, an important pier for embarkation and disembarkation of passengers and goods in the city of Mumbai. My dad had sold postcards to tourists at the Gateway and then spent his rupees on the most delicious bhel puri, Bombay's noted street food. My aunty would meet up with her friends on Marine Drive and on special occasions go for afternoon tea at the Taj Palace.

Schools at first were in Colaba and then in Byculla. Pune was where they visited their grandparents and Juhu beach was where they partied as teenagers. All these names and places were talked about frequently and I was more familiar with them than the names of the surrounding English towns where I was born.

Virtually everyone that visited our home spoke with the same accent as my family, with an Anglo-Indian lilt or, as my family described it, 'Bombay Welsh'. As a young child, I had so many 'aunties' and 'uncles' I thought we were related to everyone that visited. It took until I was around six years old to work out who were my AI family and who were our AI family friends. Every visit was accompanied by colourful stories of India and large dekshis of biryani. My school friends definitely did not have dekshis, biryani or loads of aunties and uncles at their dining room tables. I never questioned this difference; I had an innate acceptance that though born in the UK, I would ever be the child of Bombayites, and this ran deep.

News from Bombay came frequently; it seemed we had as many AI friends there as in the UK. None of my family ever went back for a visit, but home was carried in their hearts and in their souls; they believed the Bombay of their birth was not the Mumbai that now existed. Sadly, it wasn't until after their deaths, that I, along with my children and my grandchildren, joyfully and emotionally retraced their steps.

Whilst Mumbai is without a doubt more densely populated, we walked the same pathways and entered the same buildings. With every step, I felt I had been there before, so strongly ingrained were my inherited memories.

First I visited their schools; The Cathedral & John Connon School in Colaba, the Convent of Jesus & Mary in Fort, and Christ Church School in Byculla. Chowpatty beach, where they would share the 'best ever' pani puri… I even saw my grandfather's workplace at the Telegraph Office near Flora Fountain. Crawford Market where my grandmother shopped… I discovered Leopold's, Café Mondegar and the Taj Palace where they socialised. I found Bowen Memorial where they worshipped and St. Thomas Cathedral where my dad was a chorister. Their home at Abu Bakr Mansions on Apollo Bunder…

And of course, the Gateway of India.

Now a mixed-media artist, Lyn Tyler was born and grew up in the Midlands, UK. As a child of Anglo-Indian parents, her early influences – the rich mix of colours, characters, and stories, alongside a deep sense of hidden identity – are a constant thread throughout her work. Lyn uses family photos and memorabilia in her artwork, combining these with her drawings, her paintings, and her photography. Much of the work she creates tells stories of a family, an era, and a child – where two worlds meet.

*An Anglo-Indian woman
who also happens to be Lyn's aunty!*

8.

The London-based Anglo-Indian Brothers by Keith and Philip Alexander

My name is Keith, and I was born in Jaipur, Rajasthan on 22nd June 1951 to Constance and Vernon Alexander.

Five generations of my father's family served the Maharajahs of Jaipur in their State Military Forces. They were of Scottish decent, and I believe, through the generations, married local women.

My mother, Constance May Griffiths, was Welsh and was taken to India at the age of five by her father (my grandfather) who fell in love with India while serving there in the First World War. My grandfather, Thomas Henry Griffiths, refused to return when some of his children came to live in the UK, and subsequently passed away in Poona (now Pune) in the 1960s. He was responsible for starting and running the famous Kirkians hockey team while he was a senior manager in the Ammunition Factory in Kirkee, now known as Kirki.

Sport was my background from both my mother's and father's side; my father, Vernon, being the best all-round sportsman in the country which involved cricket, hockey, football, tennis and billiards.

My father won the famous Aga Khan Hockey Tournament for the BB&CI Railways. After that accomplishment, the Commissioner of Bombay Police offered him a post in the Bombay Police. That is when I transferred from Jaipur to Bombay.

After the Indian Independence, many of the Anglo-Indians left the police and joined the oil companies such as Burmah Shell, Caltex and other organisations as Chief Security Officers.

With my father having to travel around India for his job in the police, I spent three years as a day scholar at Christ Church High School in Byculla. Following the possibility of my father having to travel again, my parents decided to put my two younger sisters and myself into boarding school, St. Peter's High School, Mazagaon in Bombay.

It was here that my sporting career started. Sport was compulsory at St. Peter's, where I participated in athletics, football, hockey and gymnastics. Besides being part of the school's football, hockey and cricket teams, I also played adult football at 16 for a third division team called Matharpacady. It was there that my father was asked if I would join one of the oldest and most famous Bombay teams, the ICL (India Culture League). After finishing school, I got a job with Mahindra & Mahindra played first division hockey for them, but I also continued playing football for ICL.

In 1971, I made the Indian under-21 team for the Asian Youth Championships in Tokyo. I was only called to the trials after walking into the Cooperage Football Ground to check why the floodlights were on when the season was over. To my surprise, there were two teams playing and when I asked the groundsman what was going on, he told me it was the training camp for the selection of the under-21 team. I was a bit taken aback as I had finished joint top scorer in the first division with 23 goals but knew nothing of the trials!

While watching the game, I noticed two other players from Bombay on the pitch. I was just walking into the Western India Football Association offices to ask how players were selected for the trials, when *The Times of India* sports reporter Mr Bhaskaran approached me.

"Alexander, how old are you?" he asked me.

"I am 20 years old, Sir," I replied.

"Why are you not in the trials?" he asked.

"That is what I am going to ask the President of the WIFA!" I replied.

He then said to me, "I know you live quite close so could you go home and get some photographs, please?"

That is just what I did!

The next day in the *Evening Standard* newspaper was a picture of me with the headline "Keith Alexander Merits Trial in Indian Youth Camp." The following morning, my brother received a telegram and read it to me, saying I had to report to the two coaches, the late Mr P.K. Banerjee and Mr Gulam Basha, the next morning at 7 am. The rest is history.

I began getting very disillusioned after my return from Tokyo. I had asked some questions regarding allowances which with hindsight I should have remained quiet about, but we Anglos were always brought up to speak your mind if you feel you have been wronged. This made me make up my mind as I had recently got married, had a young daughter, and was being singled out by football officials. I decided to join my elder brother and sister who had settled in the UK.

I left for England in September 1975 and within months I realized I had made the right decision. I started working for my brother, Philip Alexander, who managed a pub and 18 months later the brewery offered me my own pub to manage. I worked for Bass Charrington, which was the biggest brewery in the UK at the time.

I enjoyed 10 great years in the pub trade and when my wife became wearied with pub life, I then joined Hambro Life Assurance as an Assistant House Manager, progressing to become the Buildings and Facilities Manager. After 27 years' service, I was made redundant after Zurich Life took us over.

I then joined the government as a Buildings Officer looking after five buildings for the Probation Service. After six years, their part of the service was privatised so I decided to retire. I bought a small apartment in Goa in 2009 and make regular trips to the motherland. Having retired, I had time to play a lot more cricket, playing for the Middlesex County's over-50s team.

Having done well as a wicketkeeper opening batsman, I was selected for England's over-60s team to play against Australia, making me probably the only person to represent two different countries at two different sports 40 years apart, which would have made my father very proud if he were alive to witness it! A bonus to this is I have now been called up for selection for the England over-70s cricket team in 2022!

Not bad for an old Anglo having also played semi-professional football when I came to the UK and second division hockey for Tetley Lions where I felt I was back home with me being the only non-Sikh of the 11 players. I think there is an irony to this when you go back to the days when the roles were reversed and there were more Anglo-

Keith Alexander

Indians in the Indian teams of the glorious years of Indian hockey.

Following on from my achievements and making a better life for my family and myself, even more of a success story is that of my older brother, Philip.

Philip came to the UK first and made it his mission to get the rest of the family across.

Unlike my sisters and I, who had a decent education, Philip unfortunately had a serious accident when he was knocked over by a car at seven years old, resulting in serious injuries. He recovered well but shortly after, he started having seizures generally at the latter stages of his school day and at home in the evenings. My parents were advised that Philip should be home taught without pressures of school life and exams. He had no educational background but and even with the backlash of Independence, he still managed to work hard and emigrate to the UK in the early 1970s.

Philip lived in North London while working as a factory machine operator. On his small wages, he still managed to send money home and help with the cost of educating his siblings. After working for a year at the factory, he changed jobs and became a barman in a pub, then worked his way up to become the manager. Not only the manager, but one of the top managers in the country for the brewery Bass Carrington. He was with the company for 40 years.

It was while Philip was running the Old Circus pub about 30 years ago that he was attacked by two thieves on his way to the bank with the weekend takings. He had about £4,000 in the plastic bag under his arm. A knife was pulled on him, but he did not let go of the money. Then one of his arms was slashed by one of the thieves, who grabbed the money and ran off. Philip chased after him and cornered him in a dead-end alleyway. Luckily, a customer witnessed this and as luck would have it, lived next door to the pub. Incredibly, her father was a police dog handler. She called her dad and he ran out with the dog to arrest the thief.

As his brother, it makes me very proud that Philip's actions resulted in getting a Police Bravery Award which was presented to him by His Royal Highness Prince Charles at Goldsmiths Hall in the City of London in the earlier 1990s.

This is just a short account of yet another Anglo-Indian that achieved something abroad. The Anglo-Indian is a breed apart that can turn his/her hand to anything and make a success of it no matter where in the world we choose to settle.

*Philip Alexander pictured with
Prince Charles at the award ceremony*

9.

An Anglo-Indian in the True North by Lesley-Anne Raymer

W hile I have chosen to describe my experiences in Canada through the words of Maud, they are my experiences. Neither Maud nor Hannah actually exists but I felt that creating them is the best way to get my story across.

"Anglo-Indian women were India's first feminists!" declared 70-year-old Maud Nailer to her granddaughter, 19-year-old Hannah. Hannah opened her big brown eyes wide in surprise and scribbled something in her notebook. The conversation was taking place in Toronto, Canada where 19-year-old Hannah was "interviewing" her grandmother for a university project on her family's experience when they arrived in Canada as immigrants.

Hannah did not know how her grandmother's statement related to the interview, but she decided to humour her and so asked, "Why do you say that? How did that make a difference to your experiences when you arrived in Canada?"

"Well, the very qualities that Anglo-Indian women possess – their self-confidence, ability to speak up and stand up for themselves, willingness to work hard, refusal to be bullied by anyone whether it be husband, in-laws, or society, coupled with their charm, good looks, and *je ne sais quoi* – these very qualities that caused them to be labelled 'fast' or 'too free' to many in Indian society, worked to their advantage in a country like Canada.

"Furthermore, as Anglo-Indians with a racial foot in two very different cultures, they were used to dealing with figurative finger-pointers, misunderstanding of their attitude towards life, disapproval in conservative India of the way they conducted themselves, such as dressing in a 'Western' way, dating whomever they wished and choosing their own husbands, not waiting for their parents to arrange a marriage for them… All these qualities, which in India were used to smear them and label them 'fast' or worse, actually worked for the average Anglo-Indian woman when she immigrated to Canada."

Hannah wasn't quite sure how to respond to this very long answer, but she tried to get the interview back on track. "Okay, but tell me about your experiences when you arrived in Canada. What were the challenges you faced and how did you deal with them?"

Maud thought back to her arrival in Canada almost 30 years ago and tried to remember how she felt at that time. "In many ways, Canada was a pleasant surprise in that the overt racism that seemed to plague the UK, which at that time was where most Anglo-Indians headed, was not so obvious in Canada. It was also a bit of a relief to arrive in a country where you felt you were free to live your life as a liberated woman. We did face challenges and bigotry, but it was more a result of 'ignorance' and 'laziness', for want of better words, rather than actual racism.

"You see," continued Maud, "until the 1970s, Canada did not have a policy of multiculturalism, so the average white Canadian had very little knowledge of other cultures. Since then, with large numbers of immigrants from almost every corner of the world and with a policy of encouraging immigrants to maintain their culture, the average Canadian, at least those in the big cities, has been exposed to different religions, different races, different cultures and, most importantly, different cuisines. Unfortunately, that has not been good for Anglo-Indians as a distinct culture."

Hannah was intrigued. "Why do you say that, Granny? Surely it is a good thing that Canada is so open and multicultural?"

Maud detected a hint of a challenge in Hannah's tone and a hint of disapproval. Maud smiled inwardly at this bright, beautiful, articulate and slightly woke granddaughter of hers. Like so many of her generation, she was a product of the Canadian university system which somehow did not encourage deep-thinking, questioning, or debate of complex issues. An education system that seemed to have failed a generation of young Canadians and produced a narrow, judgemental attitude to anything that did not conform to the dictates of certain woke rules. She was thankful that Hannah was more intelligent than the average university student and had more common sense than to simply accept shallow, convenient morals and values. Still, Hannah did tend to pounce on what she considered a flaw in the argument or, perhaps, that was just her journalistic way.

Fixing Hannah with a beady eye, Maud said, "The issue I have with this sudden avalanche of multiculturalism is that in many ways it has resulted in people being placed into certain 'cultural boxes'. Huge swathes of the globe are divided into 'areas' based on their geographical location and if you come from that area, then certain cultural and religious characteristics are assigned to you.

"For example, in Canada, anyone from India, Pakistan, Bangladesh and Sri Lanka are placed into the cultural box labelled 'South Asians'. The average Canadian (and that now includes not just white Canadians but Canadians of all races) then assigns certain broad cultural and religious values such as anyone of South Asian origin must automatically be either Sikh, Hindu or Muslim. If she is a woman, then her parents arranged her marriage and paid a dowry for her, she is kept in the kitchen all day making roti, mostly cooks biryani or samosa, and other ethnic Indian food, and so on."

"But, Granny," protested Hannah, "there are similarities in cuisine, colour and so on in people who come from that area. Why does it bother you so much?"

"As you can imagine, Hannah, for an Anglo-Indian woman who was judged in India for not being all the above, to suddenly be placed into a box with those assigned cultural characteristics, is anathema. I cannot even tell myself that the lack of understanding of the various nuances of people from those very diverse cultures is a result of racism, as I do not believe it is. I believe it is the result of laziness and a complete disinterest in anything too complicated. The average Canadian employer, colleagues and sometimes even friends seem afflicted by a complete lack of interest in understanding the different cultures that reside in the South Asian box. The more ignorant ones believe that my English was learned in Canada and that I converted to my Catholic faith after I arrived in Canada. They are not interested in knowing about Anglo-Indian culture, religion, our distinctive cuisine, our race that was deliberately created by the British when they paid their soldiers to marry Indian women to have a community within India, their 'Jewel in the Crown', that were Christian, Westernized and with English customs."

"Well, Granny, why don't you just tell people about Anglo-Indians?" said Hannah.

"I tried, my dear. Repeatedly, I have tried to educate the average Canadian about our community. Being Canadian, they listen politely; some look disbelieving when I tell them that my first language is English, that because of Anglo-Indians, English is listed as one of the many 'mother tongues' in India. Most cannot envision it when I tell them that my school was like the school in the Harry Potter books – minus the magic, of course, and the castle! It is the only way I can make people understand my British-based education, where Anglo-Indian schools are run like British schools, where we learned the best of British values (although many negative British traits also showed up), where we were taught to compete in everything but with honour and fairness. Unfortunately, even those people who do seem to understand what I was talking about in the moment, soon forgot and I was placed back into the South Asian cultural box.

"Do you know how exhausting it is to explain yourself repeatedly?" Maud continued. "Worse though was the ignorance of other Indians in Canada. I know of an Indian professor in a university who was teaching World History/Cultures. One of the students asked if at the time of the British Raj in India whether British men intermarried with Indian women. This professor had no knowledge of Anglo-Indians and simply stated that British men did 'mingle' with Indian women of loose morals. To think that someone from India, a university professor, who is supposed to be educated, could make such an ignorant statement! I was truly shocked when I heard the story and wanted to contact that professor to suggest she educate herself about Anglo-Indians."

"Okay! Tell me about your experiences in the workplace. Canada has strict rules on workplace behaviour so that everyone feels included and treated equally," declared Hannah.

"You are right. Although that wasn't always the case, and even with the strict rules there are still people who find a way to display bigotry and racism in the workplace. I used to work with a woman who referred to me as 'Paki' behind my back, and to my face took great pleasure in mocking and denigrating the Catholic Church. I could understand her anger towards the Catholic Church; she was a lesbian and felt that the Catholic Church was too judgemental towards the gay community.

"What I did not understand was her racism and bigotry. As someone from a group that had been marginalised and discriminated against in the past, I thought she would refrain from such behaviour herself. It shocked me a bit and opened my eyes to the fact that people from historically marginalised groups are also capable of being just as cruel towards someone of a group they do not like. With this particular woman, it was obvious that she did not like South Asians (that box again) and Catholics."

Hannah's eyes were like saucers. She had never heard about this from her granny. "What did you do? Did you report her to management?" asked Hannah.

"No," said Maud. "My Anglo-Indian pride kept me from doing that. My generation do not accept victimhood and I was not going to become a victim by complaining to management. I was not going to let this woman know she had offended me, as that was her intention and would have given her great pleasure. She was a very angry person. Instead, I pretended not to notice her behaviour until one day she felt the need to 'up the game' so to speak."

"What did she do?!" asked Hannah, obviously expecting some dramatic showdown.

"Nothing dramatic. She and another woman in the office, who also did not like South Asians, began a conversation with me. They told me that a fish and chips shop close to our office had been bought up by an Indian. They 'sweetly' said it was odd to see an Indian cooking fish and chips and they felt the food would not be the same.

"Just as 'sweetly', I reminded them that cooking fish and chips depends on ensuring that the batter is just right and the oil is at the right temperature. I assured them that compared to the complexity of Indian cooking which required knowledge, not just of the right batter and the temperature of the oil but also dozens of spices and the myriad ways they could be used, using a range of cooking methods unheard of in Canada, they need not fear that the Indian man at the fish and chips shop would not be able to cook the food properly!"

Hannah was chortling. She knew her granny was feisty, but she had never heard such details.

By this time, Maud was well into her story and went on to tell Hannah that this same woman made sure to tell her that if the Catholic Church wanted to keep people in the fold, then it would need to change its stance on homosexuality.

Hannah was shocked. "Did she really say that to you, Granny? And in the office?"

"She certainly did but by this time I was ready for her attacks, so I simply responded that the Catholic Church is not like a country club where it can simply change the rules to suit the clientele. It stood for the Word of God which did not change, despite man-made laws and the demands of society."

Hannah looked down at her notes. Seeing that Maud was tiring, she decided to go on to another area she wanted to know about. "So, Granny, does that mean you did not have any white Canadian friends and only mixed with Anglo-Indians or other Catholics from India?"

"Not at all. I found many fine friends amongst Canadians of all races, but I feel like I am coming home whenever I am with Anglo-Indians at the Anglo-Indian picnics and dances that the Anglo-Indian Association organises. It is such a relief not to explain what I mean when I use words like 'bugger', 'bouzard', 'Pi', 'meat safe', 'Doll' or other Anglo-

Indian words and expressions. The friendship amongst all races is there, but simply on a different level and I am content with that."

Maud smiled and went on. "I must also tell you about the little things in Canada that every new immigrant experiences. For example, until I arrived in Canada, I never referred to the washroom as that. It was always either the toilet, the cloakroom or the loo. Once when I was in Zellers, I needed to use the facilities, so I approached a young man and asked him where the toilet was. He looked blank so I mentioned that I needed the cloakroom. His face cleared and he willingly led me to the clock section of the store!

"Learning to communicate using Canadian English was part of the immigration package and led to many amusing situations. Even spelling is a little different. I used to work in aviation and part of my job was purchasing parts for the aircraft. I will never forget when I put down 'aircraft tyres' on the requisition slip, and the manager changed it to 'aircraft tires'. Using the word rubber rather than eraser has also caused many smiles.

"And, of course, the Canadian winter is something no one can anticipate. It took me a long time to get used to wearing thick coats, boots, hats, woollen scarves and mitts to cope with the outdoors, only to remove all of them when you entered someone's home. Removing your shoes and walking around in socks in someone's home kind of ruins the outfit you are wearing. Further, those warm hats simply did not support the hairstyle I used to have, so I had to change it. After the initial shock, I came to enjoy the four distinct seasons that Canada has, especially fall and winter."

"One last question. If you could do it over again, would you choose Canada?" asked Hannah.

Maud was very emphatic. "My answer to that is a resounding yes. I believe that Canada is the best country in the world. I have no regrets about moving to Canada and despite all my little grumbles above," Maud said with a sweet smile on her face, "I would choose Canada again in a heartbeat. As a member of a very tiny group (worldwide there are approximately 300,000 Anglo-Indians), no matter where we are, we face challenges to maintain our identity. But now I have you, my darling granddaughter to carry the torch, maintain our culture, and keep the memories."

Being a born diplomat, Hannah simply smiled at her granny and kissed her goodnight.

Lesley-Anne Raymer

10.

An Anglo-Indian from the USA by Blair Williams

I am an Anglo-Indian from Chennai (Madras). My grandfather, Alfred Robert Williams, whose birth certificate is dated 26th May 1880, was born in the town of Holbeach in Lincolnshire, in the UK. He was posted to India as a Tommy (foot soldier) in 1900. Released from the army, he joined the Madras Police Force around 1905 and married my Anglo-Indian grandmother. My father, Clarence, was born in 1907 and after being educated in Lovedale, Nilgiris, he joined the Indian Post and Telegraphs Department in 1935 and married my Anglo-Indian mother in 1937. I was born in 1938.

Anglo-Indians in India had distinct advantages: they had to have a male progenitor of European (usually British) heritage. They received preferential education in Anglo-Indian schools and had reserved employment in the Armed

Forces, Indian Railways, Customs Department, and the Posts and Telegraphs Department. The community was endogamous, with the women marrying only Englishmen or other Anglo-Indians; they were 100% Christian, spoke only English, and had little or no knowledge of Indian religions or languages. They were a closed, unique and independent community who considered England as their 'home'.

I received an English education in high school and college and achieved good grades. However, our curriculum didn't feature much about the geography, religion or culture of India – it was all England-related.

While in college, I sat competitive exams for Central Government Class I Railway Service. About 10,000 applicants vie for 10 to 20 positions in the Indian Railway School of Mechanical Engineering at Jamalpur, Bihar. I was selected, and, given the odds, I consider I was extremely fortunate. I was awarded a paid apprenticeship for four years. I also graduated from the Institution of Mechanical Engineers in London with a degree in Mechanical Engineering. During these years, as all my colleagues were Indians from various communities, I learned about the religion and culture of India.

I left Jamalpur as an Assistant Mechanical Engineer (AME) at the age of 24. Four years later, I was promoted to a Divisional Mechanical Engineer (DME). Around this time, I met and married Ellen Gardner, who hailed from the very prestigious and established Gardner family.

Our wedding, 1961

At this officer level, there were few Anglo-Indians, most of them being in supervisory or artisan roles. I worked in various management capacities in the Indian Railways for about 15 years. Class I gazetted positions were created by the British for privileged Indians and Englishmen and we were imbued with enormous power and prestige. Known as 'sahibs' or squires, we led a life of comfort, entitlement and ease. We had servants to do the cooking, the gardening and cleaning our homes. Our 'Officers Only' clubs had bearers to wait upon its members like myself, and among other sports, we enjoyed tennis, billiards and card games. I sometimes find it hard to believe that we could have been so privileged. I was the only young Anglo-Indian in this cadre but there were a few older Anglo-Indians who had risen to officer positions after many years of service.

Blair

In the 1970s, I was in a very eminent position as Deputy Director Inspection and Liaison with the Railway Board. It occurred to me that even though I had a significant prestige, I could never be financially independent, as although government jobs gave one privilege and power, they offered relatively little pay.

At this time, large numbers of Anglo-Indians were migrating to Australia which had by then dropped their 'whites only' policy. Prior to that in the 1950s, a huge number of the community had left for England (which they regarded as 'home').

I applied for immigration to Australia and was accepted, but, as fate would have it, at this time the United States Department of Labor put out a circular that they were short of engineers and qualifying engineers would be given a special preference to immigrate to the USA. I applied promptly and was accepted, so I completed the required medicals and received my 'green card'. This document isn't easy to obtain – millions try, and the current waiting time is 12 years! But after taking long leave from the Indian Railways, my wife and I migrated to the USA.

The USA was a huge cultural shock. Attitudes like the dignity of labour, boss-worker relationships, and the value of individuality in terms of independent opinions and outlook were new experiences. Day-to-day conveniences – i.e., the abundance and variety of food, the range of affordable housing, ease of transportation, and comfortable living standards – were a huge contrast to anything we had experienced in India.

During my first few years, I completed an MBA from Loyola University in Chicago, which gave me local accreditation, and I was fortunate enough to join the Pullman Company, a well-established firm in Chicago, who were building railcars. I fitted right in. I did not suffer any discrimination in regard to colour or race – and was treated with respect as "one of the boys"!

I was sent to inspect Pullman British subsidiaries in Britain. It brought with it the realisation that in the 1980s in the UK there was still prejudice, particularly towards coloured people from India, Pakistan and the Indies. It led me to coin a phrase: "In the UK to be white is good; in the USA to be black is bad!" As a result, I felt very fortunate that I had emigrated to the USA rather than England. My regret is that I did not try to find my relations in UK.

Over time, I had several engineering jobs in the USA, all at the managerial level, and learned how systems worked. Americans were practical and very hard workers. Qualifications such as inherited status were irrelevant (as compared to Europe), and the whole country operated on a meritocracy based on achieving efficient productivity. The main motivator was money, and middle-class Americans worked well, earned, and spent money, and generally enjoyed life. I soon eased into the role of a middle-class American and enjoyed the benefits of comfortable living and the pleasure of travelling, entertaining and being entertained.

Notwithstanding that, I never forgot the reason I came to the USA (to be financially independent) and lived frugally, saved money and prudently invested in the stock market. In 1978, after two years of living in the US, I'd figured that I needed $500,000 by 1988 to be able to exercise my options of what to do, where to live, how to entertain myself, and so on. Of course, this amount would not have been adequate to meet these requirements, and I revised my goal aiming for a million dollars by 1998 when I would be 60 years old. I achieved this ambition and began to enjoy life without the burden of being forced to find work. I could luxuriate in the freedom of choosing a job that was fulfilling and relatively free of stress. I eventually retired in 1999 and joined New York University as an Industry Professor. The salary was less, but I had much more freedom and I enjoyed teaching.

Around this time, I gave some serious thought as to what my life was about and what I really wanted to achieve. I visited India in 1998 and was taken around slums in Calcutta where many Anglo-Indians lived. I was appalled at the subhuman conditions. Moved deeply by this, I couldn't help but think: "There but for the grace of God, go I." Sending an annual donation was not a sufficient answer. I came back to the USA and spent the next few months setting up a not-for-profit organisation. (In the USA, this is called 501(c)(3), which entitles donors to receive a tax deduction from the Internal Revenue Service.)

Thus, the Calcutta Tiljallah Relief was born. The registered purpose of the charity was 'To help less fortunate Anglo-Indians in India'. I started to use the initials CTR to avoid donors thinking that the charity only helped Calcutta. Over the next few years, as I travelled around the world, I set up branches of CTR in Australia, the UK, Canada and the east and west coasts of the USA.

Canada held the first CTR fundraising dinner dance in 1998 and have since had one every year (except during the Covid-19 menace in 2020 and 2021). The west coast of the USA (Santa Clara) set up an organisation in 1990 and have been very active.

Today, CTR has centres in Canada, the UK and, of course, the USA – East and West – and sends around $60,000 to $70,000 to seven projects in India. CTR has two main thrusts: (1) providing monthly pensions to poor AI seniors, which covers about 350 recipients in six cities across India; and (2) helping educate poor AI children, which benefits about 250 children across five cities. A very rewarding activity and I feel blessed. The website is www.ctrcharity. org The charity raises money from donors mainly from the USA and Canada.

I also began to think about how posterity would view the Anglo-Indian community. There were several books/papers written about the Anglo-Indian community by English and Indian authors. Most of them evoked stereotypical images of the community i.e. women of easy virtue and men who were lazy drunkards. I wanted to create a third and more accurate point of view – one that described the community by its own members or by those who knew them well.

Accordingly, I set up a system of deciding on a theme, advertising it on the web and inviting members to contribute an article of around 3,000 words. I appointed a panel of five multinational judges, who reviewed the articles after I had removed the email reference. About 40 entries were selected. Finally, I had an editor (a well-known Anglo-Indian writer) to finalise the submissions.

I then sent the collection to a printing company and there it was! A book on Anglo-Indian culture and lifestyle. The whole process took about a year. From 2000 to 2012, under the banner of CTR, eight books were published and registered in the US Library of Congress and featured in a special section of the Calcutta Central Library where the DeRozio Center for Anglo-Indian Studies was set up in 2013. Now we had a third point of view, written by Anglo-Indians and those who knew them well. What a unique collection of the values and lifestyles of a community that is on the verge of extinction. The books will serve as source material for researchers in the future who may want to understand how the community lived before and after Indian Independence.

Today I am content. The charity CTR still operates and the books have gone out to about one thousand readers around the world. The website www.ctrcharity.org is also quite active. I've also set up a trust in India (Pondicherry) called the Blair & Ellen Williams Foundation for the higher education of Anglo-Indians. I want to seed it with enough capital so that the interest can educate about 20 students at a time. It started functioning in 2019.

I am an octogenarian and reflect a lot on my life. As you have no doubt observed, I have been singularly fortunate and extremely lucky. I believe that what one does in life is determined by ability (genes), effort and luck (about a third of each), and I may have had more than my share of good fortune! I am proudest of setting up the CTR charity, publishing the books on Anglo-Indian culture, and creating the Blair & Ellen Williams Foundation.

There is a quotation that I have used to guide my life. It goes like this:

"I am what survives me"

Erik Erikson

11.

Andrea Malam BEM – The Philanthropist

This is the story of a woman striving and learning to be a strong woman. That is what I wanted because everyone deserves a strong one in their lives. "And yes, let it be me. But it can be you too!"

I am an ordinary woman doing extra-ordinary things – an honourable woman saving and building dreams.

I often get asked about myself. This elicits a question I then like to ask myself.

Who am I?

What does achievement mean to me?

Thirty years ago, I set off from India to the United Kingdom on a journey I never thought I would take. But I did!

In search of my Purpose!

In search of my Passion!

In search of my Dream!

And years later, I am living my dream, on my terms, my rules! Carry on and you will see the light at the end of the tunnel, they say!

I have always been a woman of intentions and goals. I wished to travel across the world and visit the Seven Wonders that have made a home on this planet. My vision aims at serving mankind and inspiring the rest of humanity to live life the way I do and carry out what appears on their vision board.

Let's talk about what happened to me to enable you to see how lessons propel you forward.

I was hitting a wall. Isn't that what they say?

We were 20 miles in, and my head was screaming at me to stop. Yet somehow, my legs seemed to be carrying me forward. What was happening? Where was I?

I was doing the 26.2-mile London Marathon in April 2005. I could not have imagined doing it as I did not believe I could do it. I was almost 40 years old and had never run before that. So, what was it that made me say yes when a running group asked if I would join them one day?

We were training for the London Marathon and raising funds for a charity. My coach at that time, the wonderful Mr Piyush Gudka, said to me, "Andrea, just remember that 50% is mindset. It's all in your mind. Your aim is to finish it and not worry about how long it takes. Once you understand that, then the rest should be easy!"

So, I did not look back. I did not look at the watch. I started running forward. I had something I believed in. And when you have something you believe in, you have the motivation.

Crossing the finish line after that first marathon was both the most painful and exciting experience of my life. My family was there cheering me on, and the supporters were pushing me to the finish line.

That was the beginning of a lifelong passionate adventure of making a difference for the next generation. Each time, it was different and more challenging. Fundraising changed the way I saw the world. It changed the course of my life. Even my children understood my desire to bring about change.

I realised that one person can make a difference. We should never give up as one does not know what is around the corner. My personal fundraising continued, alongside my volunteering work with charities and non-government organisations.

October 1992: The year I got married to a British Indian, Sanjay Malam. Even before I married, it was a task to change the perception and understanding his family had with regards to me being an Anglo-Indian!

One of the biggest joys over the years has been holding my children in my arms after giving birth. The feeling of sheer happiness.

March 1994: A year of both joy and sadness! The year I had my first child, a son called Sharm. This same year I also lost my father, Wallace Alexander.

June 1996: Again, a year of both joy and sadness. The year my second child was born, a daughter named Sheena. This is also the year I lost my mother, Phyllis Alexander.

They were married for over 40 years but died within just 18 months of each other.

As a family, we have had our ups and downs. But my role as a woman, wife, mother and daughter in the family always seemed to carry many cultural burdens. Nobody asked how I was feeling. They just needed me to be strong – and that was it.

Our thoughts create feeling, feeling creates action, action creates habits. It's like a circle.

We make our own choices based on how we feel which has been stored in our subconscious.

At a very young age, I faced the death of my brother Mark, who was a victim of mistaken identity, just after his 18th birthday. He died on Friday 13th March 1980. Wrong time; wrong place.

Culture and religion played a very big part in this incident. Mark would never show pain. He was strong – not just physically, but emotionally too. Was this the reason Mark's treatment was delayed? And the internal bleeding, the cause of his death the next morning? Mark's death was a turning point for my whole family. Despite catching the culprit and sentencing him for life, my dad was unable to make peace with what had happened.

With both my other brother Geoffrey dying of terminal illness, as well close friends, and further trauma in the family, it made me realise I had a choice. Either I will be the strong one or I will become a victim of circumstances. And there was no way of going there because I realised I could be the strong one and it followed that from being the strong one, I could support others too. I do not have to prove to myself I am the strong one, but I want to be the shoulder and someone others can stand on and grow.

I was close to people suffering from terminal illnesses and knowing they had not long to live. I had supported family and friends through the journey of the inevitable. Who would be there to support them? When one is ill, the whole family needs care. Those who get left behind continue to suffer, and yet often shy away from help. I could help and support others going through the same experience. So, I reached out into the wider community, not just locally but internationally too.

I realised I had a niche – empathy. Empathy is an enormous concept. I taught myself to be better at empathy. To use empathy effectively, you need to put aside your own viewpoint and see things from the other person's perspective. Then, you can recognise behaviour that appears at first sight to be over-emotional, stubborn or unreasonable as simply a reaction based on a person's prior knowledge and experiences. The knowledge you gain from empathy can help you to use appropriate non-verbal communication.

I had finally found what was missing around me. Empathy focuses on the other person's perspective. Empathy is not an opportunity to make the conversation about you. Empathy helps the other person to relate to you on a basic human level. Find the people who want to connect with the real you. When you understand what someone else is thinking or feeling, it becomes easier to interact with them.

I experienced many biases at work. There was a huge focus on rank and grade in the civil service. This was one of the exchanges I experienced.

"It'll sound better coming from me." The woman tried not to sound condescending. I stared at her blankly. "If I say something to them, they might take more notice," she concluded.

It seemed ironic to me that we were working on a project to build greater diversity in the workplace, and yet in practice my voice was not going to be heard. I decided to do something. Bring about a change in diversity.

I joined the volunteer diversity staff group, became an executive member, and graduated to being one of the chairpersons. This was the only way my voice would be heard. I started getting busy as a Workplace Support Officer, helping and mentoring other ethnic minority staff with awareness of general and mental first aid.

"I am going to start a charity," I announced one day to my family. At the age of 50, I wanted more in life. I realised my life was meant for something more and decided to pursue my undeniable passion to help underprivileged children and their families.

Everyone needs some inspiration. We are all inspired in our life by different things and in different ways. We find it in a variety of people and things. To be honest, instead of looking for a role model, I try to become one. I would love to be an inspiration for the people around me. I want to understand other people's emotions, desires and dreams.

I am passionate about making a difference to the lives of others. My mission is to help others truly believe in themselves and recognise that when they do, life is opened to infinite possibilities. Life is too short and complicated, but if we have a goal, a path, a dream, then the decisions we take are mission-critical. You just need a person whom you can trust, who can motivate and guide you to go where you want to be.

Towards the end of 2019, I became ill, collapsing on the floor. I was found by my son at home and ended up in hospital. I had to undergo surgery that meant having six months off work. This experience affected both my physical and mental health. On recovering from surgery, I managed to travel to India in March 2020 to visit my brother who was in hospital suffering from cancer, where he sadly passed on from this ravaging disease.

Yet all this pain also became my inspiration for my next calling…

… Saving Dreams.

This is a charity that I founded in 2020, and it's going places!

You can always take a chance to make that difference. You need to listen to your heart. No matter what happens, never give up on your dreams. I never did....

2020 and 2021 have been very different from the other years, with the Covid-19 pandemic affecting the lifestyle for almost every person in the world. There were total lockdowns and travel restrictions everywhere, but volunteering came naturally. I felt I needed to contribute to the wider society. It was time to hang up my work robe and support the current crises, not forgetting, of course, the Afghan and the Ukraine refugees.

I started supporting my local community as a Covid Health Champion, helping with the distribution of PPE to schools, care homes and care workers.

I also found myself supporting the Covid rapid testing and the delivery of the vaccinations at different clinics and pharmacies in London.

Then I began running a food bank collection with family and friends to help the homeless and people below the poverty line.

I have always followed my heart and 'achieved the unbelievable' as my family put it. Turning my Passion into my Purpose, I live by my word. My belief is that life matters and that it is our choice to live it to grow our dreams and complete them.

I do what I do because life matters and we need to start living, taking charge of our own power, control, authenticity and integrity to fulfil our dreams.

I am also particular about workplace diversity. To accomplish this, I work to ensure that a rich and diverse group of people of various ethnicities work within the community to accomplish the great things we plan to achieve.

Make every day an opportunity to serve others and give others happiness and joy.

What you give is what you will receive, and sometimes what you receive is more than what you give...

"Every great dream begins with a dreamer."

Harriet Tubman,
American Abolitionist
Founder of the Underground Railroad

As a multi award-winning leader and ambassador in diversity, a humanitarian, an author, and an inspirational speaker. I strongly believe in connecting, supporting, and empowering dreamers to help them achieve their dreams.

I came up with an idea, started working on it and published it!

Yes, I became a co-author in an anthology called *The New Woman* and got my biography *Saving Dreams* published.

All your dreams will come true if you have the courage to pursue and believe in yourself.

You must believe in your dreams to have them become real.

Over the years, I have achieved many important goals and received many awards. These include:

❖ publishing my biography *Saving Dreams* and being featured in *The New Woman* anthology;

❖ running marathons and climbing mountains for charity;

❖ being commended for exemplary service;

❖ featuring in many magazines and publications;

❖ winning various awards such as Women of the World Lifetime Achievement Award, NCA Diversity Role Model Award, International Women Achievers' Award, Admired Global Indians Award, Indian Achiever Form Award for Nation Building;

❖ gaining an Honorary Doctorate Of Advanced Studies;

❖ founding the Saving Dreams charity;

❖ being awarded a BEM in the 2022 Queen's New Year's Honours List for implementing change in Diversity and Inclusion across Law Enforcement.

As an avid researcher, and a woman not afraid of challenges and breaking barriers, I have over 20 years of knowledge and experience in responding to time-critical crises in an effective manner.

Be Inspired!

Be Influenced!

Be Independent!

But be You! Be Yourself! Grow your own way!

My first London Marathon in 2005

12.

The Way Forward

I acknowledge and recognise diversity is an opportunity but also a challenge. I believe it's about accepting that everyone is different, not just by virtue of their race, age, religion and gender, but because of factors such as their home culture, mannerisms and accents.

To be treated equally and respected should **never** be a privilege. It is a right. It is about mutually empowering another person with respect and appreciating what makes one different. There is so much more to do to improve Diversity, Inclusion and Equality – **together** we can make a difference.

To me, this means that I will continue to call out behaviours and actions that are unfair, discriminatory or offensive, as I strive to be a strong advocate for tackling the issues that still exist. I will consider how my role in culture change, inclusion and engagement can help make the changes we need to see.

I work with various and diverse cultures, and I don't pretend that it is easy.

Diversity may be the hardest subject to work on in the community or workplace, but it can be a collective voice and an empowerment for change.

I have tried to raise awareness of ethnic and racial bias in diversity and significantly contributed across law enforcement and other sectors to implementing change and collaborative practices, as part of leading the staff association.

The UK and India are supposedly looking to re-imagine their partnership amidst the current global realities and engagement. This is despite the many challenges, such as the pandemic and civil right issues.

Values and beliefs have changed for the better. The new generation have been left to follow the faith they choose. It has been stated that the Anglo-Indians are very large-hearted people and will not hesitate to come forward to help others.

In uncertain times, one thing we have undoubtedly seen amongst all the fear, has been kindness; kindness in the form of community support, sharing hope and positivity, raising money for organisations in need, and much more.

Kindness can transform our communities, be that in schools, places of work or within families, with the added benefit that helping others is good for your own mental health too!

There are several individuals and groups who fundraise and doing excellent work.

One such individual is Blair Williams, the founder of Calcutta Tiljallah Relief, who agreed to share his story and experience with us in his chapter. The registered purpose of the charity is 'To help less fortunate Anglo-Indians in India.'

One of the noblest missions in which an individual can be engaged is starting a charity or a non-profit account. For many, bringing improvement to the lives of those who require it can be viewed as passion. I house such a noble passion in my heart.

My personal fundraising continues, alongside my volunteering work with various charities. Having supported and helped various NGOs and charities with their projects, I decided to start up a charity, an international charity based in London called Saving Dreams.

The main objectives are to:

1. alleviate suffering and help maintain human dignity.

2. enable children to escape poverty and offer opportunities to become model citizens.

The website is www.savingdreams.org.uk

Saving Dreams currently has four trustees heading it: Keith Alexander, Conrad Vince, Sharm Malam and myself. We are always looking for more fundraisers and trustees to get involved and help us do the right thing. We work alongside other volunteers and charities in London and in Mumbai. As people of Anglo-Indian ancestry, we are proud to be influenced by other great Anglo philanthropists and fundraisers.

Saving Dreams is going from strength to strength, with donations and volunteer support in the UK, India and

Nepal. I speak from experience and sometimes it can be lonely heading up a charity, but having a great support network also plays a big part in survival. And yes, we survive, being achievers and believing in ourselves.

The photo above is children from the Seva Sangam, happy with their gifts donated through Saving Dreams. Lok Seva Sangam is a charity/NGO that supports TB and leprosy patients and their families. They also run preschool education centres for underprivileged children.

I am fulfilling my dream, walking through my life in service of others.

If I could leave my one message to my loved ones, it would be this: you can always take a chance to make a difference. To change your life, you must do it yourself, then you can believe in yourself.

To make a difference, you do not necessarily need to aim high. Focus on your community. Listen to your heart, follow your true calling, and save your dreams for a better world.

May the culture, spirit, bravery,and work ethic grow in this proud community and be passed on to the next generation.

Volunteering in a very diverse London

13.

Famed Anglo-Indians - Past and Present

It was 1991, on a fine Sunday evening, watching TV in North London with my uncle, when on came the movie *Summer Holiday* with pop star Cliff Richard. I was singing along with the songs, such as *Bachelor Boy* and *Summer Holiday*.

"Did you know that Cliff Richard is not his real name, that he is an Anglo-Indian, and was born in India?" said my uncle.

"Are you sure, Uncle?" I asked.

"Yes, my dear child. And there are other Anglo-Indians too from India in the music industry."

And that was when I started digging into all the information available on artists such as Cliff Richard.

Many Anglo-Indians left India after independence in 1947, while the 1950s, 60s and 70s saw a steady increase in the departure of many to Europe – mainly Great Britain – Canada, Australia and the USA.

There are a few names that have made a name for themselves away from their place of birth in the film and music industries such as Merle Oberon, Diana Hayden, and Engelbert Humperdinck. Some in India too, such as sports personalities Roger Binny and Leslie Walter Claudius.

In my teens growing up in India, we would love listening to pop sensations Cliff Richard, Tony Brent and Engelbert Humperdinck, but I only realised they were Anglo-Indians when I moved to the UK in my early twenties, thanks to my uncle and cousins.

Here are some examples of famous Anglo-Indians:

1. The Thomas brothers – Ryan, Adam, and Scott – Actors/Presenters

In 2019, the Thomas Brothers – Ryan (who plays Jason Grimshaw in *Coronation Street* and won *Celebrity Big Brother*), Adam (who played Adam Barton in *Emmerdale* and is a presenter on *I'm a Celebrity, Get Me out Of Here!* spin-off show *Extra Camp* set in Australia) and Scott (who finished third on the ITV2 dating show *Love Island* in 2016) – headed to India for a trip of a lifetime. They wanted to explore their family heritage in the hope of seeking out long-lost relatives. The series was called *Absolutely India: Mancs in Mumbai* and aired on ITV.

They were all born in the UK, but it was during this trip that they realised they were in fact Anglo-Indians. They were joined by their father, Dougie James, an Anglo-Indian music promoter and 1970s soul singer who used to perform with 70s band Dougie James and the Soul Train. Anyone remember them?

Dougie James died unexpectedly in November 2020, aged 72, not long after doing the reality show in India.

2. Sir Cliff Richard OBE – Singer/Actor

"The thrill of hearing your own voice recorded is still there. I still live it, going into the studio and thinking how can I sing this song, and between the producers and the musicians, you find a way of doing it."

Cliff Richard

Sir Cliff Richard was born Harry Rodger Webb in Lucknow, India in 1940. His father was British, and his mother was an Indian-born Brit. In 1948, following Indian independence, the family embarked on a three-week sea voyage to Tilbury, Essex, England aboard the S.S.

Ranchi. In the 1950s, Webb decided to change his name to Cliff Richard to boost his singing career as the lead singer of the group The Drifters. They became Cliff Richard and the Drifters, and finally changed their name to Cliff Richard and the Shadows. They appeared in six feature films, such as *The Young Ones* and, of course, *Summer Holiday*.

Over a career spanning 60 years, Sir Cliff has won countless awards and Gold and Platinum discs. More than 130 of his records have reached the UK Top 20, more than any other artist.

3. Merle Oberon - Actress

Merle Oberon was an Anglo-Indian actress born in Bombay in British India on 19th February 1911. She was probably a unique case in the history of Anglo-Indians as she gave herself a false identity to pass off as an upper crust lady. She began her career in the British film industry with the role of Anne Boleyn in *The Private Life of Henry VIII*, followed by *The Scarlet Pimpernel* and *The Dark Angel*. She also appeared as Cathy in the highly-acclaimed *Wuthering Heights* with Sir Laurence Olivier as Heathcliff in 1939.

Merle Oberon retired and moved to Malibu, California where she suffered a stroke and died in 1979, aged 68.

4. Shelley Conn - Actress

Actress Shelley Conn was born on 21ˢᵗ September 1976 in the UK. She is an Anglo-Indian actress in her own right (both parents are Anglos), as well as being the grand-niece of Merle Oberon. Shelley's work includes *Casualty*, *Merseybeat*, *Mistresses*, and most recently, the role of Mary Sharma in Netflix's *Bridgerton*.

5. Engelbert Humperdinck MBE - Singer

"I really enjoy what I do. And if you want a lasting career, you have to work at it. Keep it current. Keep it fresh."

Engelbert Humperdinck

The British pop singer Engelbert Humperdinck MBE was born Arnold George Dorsey in Chennai (formerly Madras,

British India) on 2nd May 1936. His family moved to Leicester in the UK after Indian independence.

He has been described as 'one of the finest middle-of-the-road balladeers' of all time. He released his first single *I'll Never Fall in Love Again* in 1958. He achieved international prominence in 1967, with his hit singles *Release Me* and *The Last Waltz* both topping the UK singles chart in 1967. He represented the UK in the Eurovision Song Contest in 2012. He has sold over 140 million records worldwide.

6. Diana Hayden – Actress, TV Host and Winner of Miss World 1997

"I was never considered good-looking because I was dark."

Diana Hayden

Diana was born 1st May 1973 in Hyderabad, India to Anglo-Indian parents and grew up in the cities of Hyderabad and Secunderabad in Andhra Pradesh. She is an Indian actress, television host, model, and the winner of Miss World 1997. She also won three subtitles during the pageant and is the only Miss World titleholder to do so. Following her tenure as Miss World's global representative, Hayden moved to London and studied acting at the Royal Academy of Dramatic Art. Diana is also associated with many charities and NGOs.

Diana is married to an American businessman, Collin Dick.

7. Leslie Walter Claudius - Hockey Player

The great Anglo-Indian hockey player, Leslie Claudius, was born on 25th March 1927 in Bilaspur, India. He was the first player ever to earn 100 caps and he was a member of the Indian medal-winning team in the Olympics (1948, 1952, 1956 and 1960) as well as many international tours. In 1971, he was awarded the Padma Shri, one of India's highest civilian honours. In 1978, he was appointed as the manager of the Indian team for the Bangkok Asian Games. He died after a long battle with cirrhosis of the liver in 2012.

Claudius was considered one of the all-time hockey greats. Not many people know that for the London 2012 Olympics, Bushey tube station was renamed after Claudius in the special "Olympics Legends Map".

8. Roger Binny - Cricketer

Roger Michael Humphrey Binny was a cricket all-rounder who is best known for his impressive bowling performance in the 1983 Cricket World Cup winning squad where he was the highest wicket-taker. Binny was the first Anglo-Indian to play cricket for India. He was born on 19th July 1955 in Bangalore, where he started his cricket career, and he was a right-arm fast medium bowler and a right-handed batsman.

In 2012, Binny was appointed as one of the five members of the selection panel of the Board of Control for Cricket in India. His son Stuart has followed in his footsteps, playing both state and international cricket.

8. Tony Brent - Singer

Reginald Hogan Bretagne, known as Tony Brent, was of Anglo-Indian descent. He was born on 13th August 1926, and lived in Byculla, Bombay. He was the oldest son of Patrick and Marian Bretagne and had three brothers and two sisters. Brent moved to the UK in 1947 at the age of 25. Two years later in 1949, he won a talent contest at the Regal Theatre in Kingston with his performance of *Some Enchanted Evening*. This led him to the BBC Showband, where he performed under the batons of Ambrose and Cyril Stapleton. His first hit came in 1951 with *Walking to Missouri* and his classic hits included *Cindy, Oh Cindy, Dark Moon* and *Don't Save Your Love for a Rainy Day*.

Brent left the UK in 1961 to live in Australia. He died at the age of 65 of a heart attack in Sydney in 1993, but his music still lingers on.

9. Helen - Bollywood Actress and Dancer

Helen Ann Richardson Khan, known as Helen, is an Indian Bollywood actress and dancer. Helen was born on 21st November 1938 in British Burma to an Anglo-Indian father and a Burmese mother. She has appeared in over 700 films and is known for her supporting character roles and guest appearances, in a career spanning 70 years. She has received two Filmfare Awards.

In 2009, Helen was awarded the Padma Shri, one of India's highest civilian honours. She has been an inspiration for four films and a book. Helen is married to Salim Khan, a prominent Bollywood screenplay writer, and currently lives in Mumbai. Khan already had four children from a previous marriage, but Helen has had a large role in keeping the family united.

10. Ruskin Bond - Author

Ruskin Bond is an Anglo-Indian author, born in Kasauli, Punjab States Agency, British India in May 1934. His father, Aubrey Alexander Bond, taught

English to the princesses of Jamnagar Palace, and Ruskin and his sister lived in the palace until the age of six. His father joined the RAF in 1939. When Ruskin was eight years old, his mother separated from his father and married Hari, a Punjabi Hindu. His father arranged for Ruskin to be brought to New Delhi where he was posted. When he was 10, his father died during the war while posted in Calcutta. Ruskin was at his boarding school in Shimla and was informed about this tragedy by his teacher. He was thoroughly heartbroken. Later, he was raised by his mother and stepfather who lived in Dehradun.

His first novel, *The Room on the Roof*, was published in 1956, and it won the John Llewellyn Rhys Prize in 1957. This is a prize awarded to a British Commonwealth writer under 30. He has written more than 500 short stories, essays and novels including over 50 books for children.

He was awarded the Sahitya Akademi Award (India's foremost literary honour) in 1992 , the Padma Shir in 1999 and the Padma Bushhan (India's third highest civilian honour) in 2014. He lives with his adopted family in Landour, Mussoorie.

Further Reading and Information

Websites:

www.ctrcharity.org

www.loksevasangam.org.in

www.savingdreams.org.uk

Articles:

https://theculturetrip.com/asia/india/articles/the-history-of-how-bombay-became-mumbai-in-1-minute/

Books:

Bond, Ruskin, *The Room on the Roof*, Penguin (2017)

Sharma, Ritu, *The New Woman*, Book Brilliance Publishing (2021)

Films:

Summer Holiday

Acknowledgements

I would like to thank my publishing team – Brenda Dempsey, Olivia Eisinger and Zara Thatcher – as well as my family and friends who have helped and supported me in finalising this project.

Thank you to my son Sharm and daughter Sheena. They are proud of my achievements and are always a support to me. Without them, this would not be possible.

A big thank you to Vishwajeet Deshmukh for agreeing to write the foreword, as well to all of the contributors of the book: Joseph Oliver, Richard Lloyd Raymer, Lyn Tyler, Keith and Philip Alexander, Lesley-Anne Raymer, and Blair William

Thank you!

About the Author

Andrea Malam BEM is a multi-award-winning Leader in Diversity and an international role model, who enjoys making an impact, inspiring and motivating others. She is an British Empire Medal recipient for exemplary service for her role in law enforcement protecting the public.

Andrea is the Founder Trustee of the charity Saving Dreams, which aims to help alleviate suffering alongside enabling children to escape poverty with education and support. The charity supports various projects, helping thousands of underprivileged children and their families worldwide.

Andrea is also a published author and speaker, a philanthropist, and a humanitarian, who enjoys Connecting, Supporting and Empowering Dreamers to achieve their goals.

Andrea was born Andrea Alexander in Mumbai, India to parents of British Ancestry but settled in London, United Kingdom, where she currently lives with her husband and two children.

Andrea can be contacted at connect@andreamalam.co.uk

linkedin.com/in/dr-andrea-malam-bem-b38aa313a

https://www.andreamalam.com